Le Pèlerinage
de Charlemagne

Edited by Glyn S. Burgess

Société Rencesvals British Branch
Edinburgh 1998

British Rencesvals Publications 2

Available from The Secretary
Société Rencesvals British Branch
Dr A. E. Cobby
Modern and Medieval Languages Library
University of Cambridge
Sidgwick Avenue
Cambridge
CB3 9DA

ISBN 0 9519791 3 2

Printed by Printing Services
The University of Edinburgh

Design by Kenneth Wilson

PREFACE

I first published an edition and translation of *Le Pèlerinage de Charlemagne* in 1988, in the *Garland Library of Medieval Literature* (series A, volume 47, Garland Publishing: New York and London). On that occasion the Introduction was written by Anne Elizabeth Cobby. The present edition is a thoroughly revised version of that printed in the Garland volume, and the prose translation has now become a line-by-line rendering of the text. A substantial part of the notes from the earlier volume has been reproduced here and I am grateful to Dr Cobby for allowing me to use sections of the notes which she originally helped me to draft. The Introduction to this new volume aims to offer not only the basic information required by readers of the text (manuscript, dating, sources, influences, etc.) but also a detailed reading of the text, which attempts to draw out the key issues at stake and to offer comments on the way these issues can be viewed and the conclusions which could be reached.

In preparing this volume I owe a deep debt of gratitude to Ian Short, who has acted as my editor and helped me with innumerable difficulties relating to the text and its interpretation. I have also benefited from the excellent advice and comments of Peter Ainsworth, Philip Bennett, John Curry, Jacqueline Eccles and Sarah Kay.

Glyn S. Burgess
Liverpool, June 1998

CONTENTS

INTRODUCTION

The *Pèlerinage de Charlemagne* is a tale of epic heroes, led by Charlemagne, who pay a successful visit to Jerusalem, followed by an even more successful and particularly eventful visit to Constantinople. These epic heroes are surprisingly never called upon to fight and to an exxxiitent they are characters looking for a world in which to demonstrate their heroism. Although ostensibly pilgrims, they are in fact warriors without a war, a mixture of the tourist and the thug. The focus of attention, however, is Charlemagne himself. When, at the outset, his prestige is challenged by the queen, he sets off to restore his reputation, and when the Franks are belittled by their experiences in Constantinople, a world which both impresses and disconcerts them, he leads them in the act of ritual jesting and boasting (*gaber*). This unwise act seems to stem from a sense of frustration and inadequacy. Moreover, the crucial event of this poem, the one which determines the central issues of power and prestige, occurs when, to their consternation, the Franks are called upon actually to carry out their jests. But all's well that ends well and the Franks return home in glory, armed with an abundance of holy relics, which they acquire in Jerusalem, and basking in the glow of an unexpected victory over the Emperor of Constantinople.

The most intriguing question raised by the *Pèlerinage* concerns the degree to which it can be regarded as a serious work. Is it in fact never entirely serious? 'This poet', writes Grigsby, 'has a constant twinkle in his eye, a smile on his lips, as if he, like the French in Constantinople, had just finished a satisfying meal with copious amounts of wine' ('The Relic's Rôle', p. 34). If this is so, what sort of comedy are we dealing with? Some critics use the term satire, though many others prefer to talk of parody. Brians sees the text as 'an outrageous parody from start to finish of the men and adventures of the *chansons de geste*' (p. 170).[1] Is this the view we should take of the intentions of the author of the *Pèlerinage de Charlemagne*? Or should we take a different view and see this work, for example, as a piece of political propaganda? This poem, writes Gosman, 's'insère dans une tradition

---

[1] For a recent study of parody in the *Pèlerinage* see Cobby, *Ambivalent Conventions*. See also Bonafin, *La Tradizione del Voyage de Charlemagne*, chapter 2, Neuschäfer, 'Le Voyage de Charlemagne en Orient als Parodie der *chanson de geste*', Owen, '*Voyage de Charlemagne* and *Chanson de Roland*' and Süpek, 'Une Parodie royale du moyen âge'. For full details of books and articles see the Select Bibliography (pp. li-lviii).

propagandiste au service d'une vision politique' (p. 64). For him, it deals with such issues as the desire in twelfth-century France for a renewal of the Empire (*renovatio imperii*) and for the independence of the Frankish monarchy from the papacy. Any comic elements would therefore be secondary to the text's serious political objectives. Vance views the poem as humorous, but for him it examines at the same time a number of crises in the Latin West, such as spirituality, political law and male sexual identity, ultimately demonstrating that Capetian political power is a 'tissue of illusions' (pp. 165-66, 183). Readers must make up their own minds on such matters. This Introduction will examine some preliminary issues relating to the text and then go on to provide a reading of the *Pèlerinage de Charlemagne* which aims to identify and comment on some of the problems which it raises.

The Title of the Poem

Originally untitled, like many medieval works, the *Pèlerinage de Charlemagne* is also referred to by modern editors and critics as the *Voyage de Charlemagne à Jérusalem et à Constantinople*, following the surviving *incipit* to the text. If the use of *Pèlerinage* can be justified by Charlemagne's visit to the Holy Sepulchre in Jerusalem, his visit to Constantinople is not self-evidently a pilgrimage in any but the loosest sense of the term, even though God's support for the Frankish victory does seem to give the Constantinople episode a spiritual significance over and above that of a mere journey. The important role played in the narrative by the recuperation of the holy relics is further justification for regarding Charlemagne's entire journey as a pilgrimage, though the Emperor's actual motivation for undertaking it — to repair his wounded pride — seems to undercut any idea of piety.

The Manuscript

Modern readers of the *Pèlerinage de Charlemagne* are unfortunately unable to consult even a single manuscript of the text. The sole witness to the text was MS London, British Museum, Royal 16 E VIII, which has not been seen since 7 June 1879. It had certainly been consulted and transcribed by Michel in 1836, and Koschwitz, who produced an edition of the text in 1880, reports that he based his edition both on that of Michel, which had been checked against the original by R. P. Wülcker, and on a facsimile provided by J. Koch. Michel dated the manuscript to the thirteenth century, Koschwitz to the end of the thirteenth or the beginning of the fourteenth century, while some modern editors place it firmly in the fourteenth century. Michel's edition remains useful, but modern editors have to base their own texts on Koschwitz's first edition, or on the diplomatic transcription which he includes in his later editions. The text of Koschwitz's first edition was collated with the manuscript by H. Nicol in 1881 and found to contain only a few minor errors.

The Date of the Poem

The many efforts which have been made to identify a convincing date for the *Pèlerinage de Charlemagne* have met with failure. Gaston Paris dated the text to the period before the First Crusade, placing it in the third quarter of the eleventh century. Koschwitz concluded that it dated from around the time of the *Chanson de Roland*, i.e., for him, the second half or the end of the eleventh century, while Coulet saw it as being more or less contemporary with the *Couronnement de Louis*, i.e. around 1130 or later. Aebischer confessed that he did not know the date and facetiously opted for the midpoint between the earliest and latest dates proposed, namely 1112 (p. 29). Picherit examines the rivalry between the Bishop of Paris, who in 1109 inaugurated a fair known as the *Lendit* to celebrate a fragment of the True Cross, and the monks of Saint-Denis, who had their own *Lendit* as early as 1048. He concludes that the *Pèlerinage* 'was written at some point during this long period of rivalry, which lasted from about 1109 until shortly after 1205' (p. vii, see also Bédier, IV, pp. 137-41).

A host of other dating criteria, too diverse to summarize here, has led a number of critics, including Heinermann, Frings, Caulkins, Vance and Cobby, to argue for a date of composition within the second half of the twelfth century. If for no other reason than the interesting use of the concept of courtliness in Oliver's *gab* (see below p. xxxvi), I would agree with those who date the composition of the poem to the middle of the twelfth century. Heinermann's suggestion that Louis VII and Eleanor of Aquitaine might have served as contemporary models for Charlemagne and his queen is also in my view by no means implausible.

The Structure of the Narrative

The *Pèlerinage de Charlemagne* can be divided into four unequal parts, corresponding approximately to vv. 1-97 (Introduction), vv. 98-238 (Visit to Jerusalem), vv. 239-857 (Visit to Constantinople) and vv. 858-70 (Conclusion).[2] We note immediately that, unlike many other works of its period, the *Pèlerinage* has no formal prologue. The first lines are an integral part of the story. There is no mention of a patron or a source and no use is made of the typical formulae employed at the time to capture an audience's attention. The Introduction could be further divided into the initial scene of the quarrel between Charles and his queen at Saint-Denis (vv. 1-57) and the return to Paris, which is followed by preparations for departure (vv. 58-97). Charles' decision, announced in v. 57, that he will not rest until he has seen King Hugo of Constantinople, dominates the remainder of the text. The Constantinople episode permits of several divisions, principally (a) the events which precede the *gabs* (vv. 262-445) and (b) the *gabs* themselves and their consequences (vv. 446-857). Further divisions into smaller units are possible. The Conclusion is brief, the return to France and the final events of the story being recounted very swiftly.

The poet has clearly no intention of creating a numerically balanced structure for the text, even for the two central episodes. The number of lines concerned, using the divisions suggested above, are (i) 97, (ii) 141, (iii) 619, (iv) 13, with the Constantinople episode thus taking up almost 75% of the entire narrative.

The Narrative

We must now examine how the poem develops and see how the various strands of the story are combined to create the poem in its present form. It will be seen that repetition, in both theme and language, is an important aspect of the poet's technique and that serious and comic elements rub shoulders throughout the poem.

---

[2] Vv. 98-111 (laisse VII) recount the journey from Paris to Jerusalem and act as a transition section between the first two episodes. They could therefore be said to belong to the Introduction rather than to the Jerusalem episode. Similarly, since the Franks leave Jerusalem in vv. 239-41 and first see Constantinople in v. 262, vv. 239-61 can be seen as a transition between the second and third episodes and therefore as forming part of the Jerusalem section.

(i) Introduction (vv. 1-97)

The principal characters, Charles and his wife, are introduced to us in the opening lines. Without their joint presence in the first scene and the resulting quarrel, the journey as we have it would not be motivated. The king and queen are presented as surrounded by dukes, lords, barons and knights. In the medieval world, wealth and power must be witnessed and admired, and the number and quality of one's supporters are of crucial importance as an indicator of status. The atmosphere is one of pomp and ceremony and the place is Saint-Denis, a location which enjoyed a privileged position at the time and which before the end of the twelfth century was often coterminous, in literary terms, with the national capital. The poet is stressing here the link between Crown, Sword and Church, a harmonious relationship which any medieval ruler would wish to foster and sustain. The ruler concerned may ostensibly be Charlemagne (reigned 771-814), but the values he upholds are those of the poet's own day. God is seen as supporting monarchy and conquest and the two are brought together here in ceremonial splendour. Church and ruler are united by Charles's act of crossing himself (v. 2). Had Charles been content merely to enjoy the occasion, in which he was playing a starring role, all would have been well. But vanity gets the better of him and he cannot resist seeking reassurance of his special status. He seeks it from the person best qualified to bolster his self-importance, his wife. As she is juridically his equal, her opinion carries considerable weight. Charles asks her to confirm that she has never seen anyone so well suited to the wearing of a crown and a sword (vv. 9-10), and for good measure he throws in the boast (v. 11) that he will use his lance to conquer yet more cities (thereby increasing his power and status, in accordance with his obligation as monarch).

Up to this point, the atmosphere has been entirely positive, and it could have remained so if the queen had been willing to play her part and confirm Charles's image of himself. But she refuses to fall in with the spirit of the occasion and to pander to the king's desire for self-congratulation, thereby shattering the positive atmosphere and creating a rift between herself and her husband. Her remark also suggests the possibility of a disparity between Charles as he sees himself and Charles as he really is. Whereas he regards himself as incomparable, she has the temerity to compare him unfavourably with someone else, thus creating a potentially devastating threat to his stature and status. There is no reason to think that the queen has any particular desire to vaunt the superiority of the Emperor of Greece and Constantinople, a man she had not even seen. She had merely heard tell of this king (v. 46) and had therefore no way of knowing whether his crown, when worn in the company of his knights, suited him better than that worn by her husband (vv. 13-16). When pressed on this issue by an angry Charles, she attempts to narrow down the problem to one of wealth, claiming to accept that Charles is indeed superior in prowess and knighthood (vv. 29-30) and inferior only in material wealth (v. 27). Presumably her hope is that Charles will interpret the issue of wealth as less damaging to his ego than that of his effectiveness in military matters. But this hope is soon dashed, for the damage has been done. In Charles's view, the original accusation, relating to the appearance of the two kings when surrounded by their knights, still stands, and its seriousness derives to a great extent from the presence of Charles' own men, who overheard the remark (v. 18). The queen's comment cannot therefore simply be brushed aside. Significantly, the author intervenes, calling the queen unwise and stating that when asked for her opinion she replied 'foolishly' (v. 12). In this way, the author introduces the audience to the theme of folly, which will prove to be of considerable importance at a later stage in the text.

What motivates the queen's 'foolish' attack on Charles? First, perhaps, a desire not to play the role which Charles has suddenly thrust upon her. She was chosen by her husband to act as spokesperson for the court, and for Charles it was clearly her duty as his wife to respond positively to his prompting and to lavish praise both on him and on the spectacle being created by the combination of his regalia and his persona. He was expecting from his wife both loyalty and the massaging of his ego. But his pompous language, his bragging and his wish to be seen as the perfect specimen of kingship were not to the queen's liking, so her second motivation would be an impulse to prick the bubble of his self-importance. Perhaps she has been waiting for an opportunity to compare her husband with the foreign king about whom she had heard talk (v. 45). The remark 'You think too highly of yourself' (v. 13) is probably no more than a snarl of frustration, something which was not intended to be taken too seriously.

But Charles had not expected contradiction (certainly not from his wife) and his reaction to her reproof shapes the entire plot. He is stunned by her reference to someone

who is 'more dashing' than he (v. 14) and whose crown suits him 'better' than does his own
(v. 16). He is angry at what has been said (vv. 17, 26, 30) and, because of the humiliation
engendered by this public act of defiance, he holds his head bowed low (v. 18), like
Charlemagne in the *Chanson de Roland* (vv. 214, 771). Gestures such as this take on great
significance in medieval literature and they possess symbolic value. Humiliation was not a
feeling which could be ignored and Charles naturally demands to know the name of this
superior king (vv. 19, 39). The idea, which he articulates immediately, that the two kings
will wear their crowns together (v. 20), fashions the narrative in that it anticipates an event
which will actually take place at a later, climactic point in the story (vv. 805, 809, 816-17,
822).

Aware of the enormity of her blunder, and knowing that she has unintentionally
brought shame on him (v. 38), the queen at once tries further means of extricating herself
from her predicament. It was a wifely joke, she says (v. 33), and she will undergo any form
of ordeal he imposes in order to exculpate herself (i.e. she relies on God to protect her and
confirm her innocence). She even pleads ignorance of the name of the king involved. But
this is all to no avail and she is finally forced to name the king whom she considers superior
to her husband. In a final attempt to wriggle out of this difficult situation, she affirms that,
in spite of the excellence of King Hugo's barons, Charles's men are nevertheless superior to
his (v. 50). But her ploy fails and Charles expresses his determination to discover the truth
about this king. The punishment for lying will be death by decapitation (vv. 52, 55). She
has, however, at least avoided any immediate retribution, apart from a reprimand from her
husband for having doubted his power (v. 56). The queen is left in no doubt that she is now
quite definitely in her husband's bad books (v. 54). Charles will not rest until he has seen
this king for himself.

When we reach v. 57, the story is well and truly launched and it will take the author
just over eight hundred lines to bring it to the point at which Charles can pronounce his
verdict with respect to the queen (v. 869). The second section of the Introduction is largely
taken up with preparations for departure. It introduces us to some of the characters who will
figure in the story: Roland, Oliver, William of Orange, Naimes, Turpin, etc. (vv. 61-65).
These are known to us, and no doubt to the audience, from the *Chanson de Roland* and other

chansons de geste.[3] This section of the text also contains a surprise. Instead of making an entirely truthful statement about his intentions, Charles announces to his men that they will be visiting Jerusalem to worship the cross and the altar (vv. 68-70). He claims that this visit has been forced upon him by a dream, one which he has had on three occasions (v. 71). Charles does not completely neglect to mention his wish to visit a king of whom he has heard, but he supplies no details and gives the appearance of attaching only secondary importance to this aspect of his journey (vv. 72-75). Prophetic dreams of this nature are certainly an epic phenomenon, but in this case they bear the hallmark of a cover-up for Charles's true intentions. Critics have taxed Charles with hypocrisy here. By claiming a pious motive for his departure, the king could be seen as adopting a ploy aimed at beginning the process of rebuilding his reputation even before he sets off on his journey. But the reference to dreams helps to remind the audience of Charles's close contact with God, and the link between God and Charles is evidently something which the poet seeks to promote throughout the poem. Moreover, even if the trip to Jerusalem does act as a camouflage for his real intention, the remainder of the text will show that the decision to visit Jerusalem before Constantinople was the result, if not of divine intervention, at least of royal inspiration. The visits to Jerusalem and Constantinople will turn out to be inextricably linked.

When the Franks set out, the idea of pilgrimage is very much to the fore. The poet is at pains to tell us that the Franks leave as pilgrims, carrying scrips and staffs of ash, but no weapons (vv. 79-80), the lack of which will be of significance during the Constantinople episode. One does notice, however, that the Franks ride *destrers* ('war-horses'), a term which some editors have found incongruous enough to justify emending it out of the text (see note to v. 81). The mention of a possible seven-year absence (v. 74) reminds us of the seven-year military expedition in the *Chanson de Roland* (v. 2). The Introduction ends with

---

[3] Like the *Chanson de Roland*, the *Pèlerinage* attaches a great deal of importance to the concept of the twelve peers, Charlemagne's chief warriors. But the list of peers in the two texts varies considerably. In the *Pèlerinage* the names are Roland, Oliver, William of Orange, Naimes, Ogier de Denmark, Berin / Genin (presumably the same as the Gerin of the *Roland*), Berenger, Turpin, Ernaut, Aimer, Bernard de Brusban and Bertrand. Only four of these peers are found in the *Roland* (Roland, Oliver, Gerin and Berenger). The *Pèlerinage* also has an unusual mixture of northern and southern peers (see Paris, pp. 36-38).

another scene in which Charles sees himself as playing a starring role. Gazing at the noble body of pilgrims and the eighty thousand men ahead of him, he is lost in self-admiration (v. 97). At least in his own eyes, he has recovered his equilibrium and at this stage he feels very much in control of events. If the queen intended to dent Charles's image of himself, she has blatantly failed to do so. But the poet has here drawn our attention to one of the fundamental themes of his narrative: power. This passage offers further confirmation that the concept of power is linked to display, and the association of power with numbers will also have significance later in the text (the eighty thousand Franks execute a remarkable disappearing trick throughout the remainder of the poem).

Another important theme elaborated in the Introduction is that of wealth. Gold is mentioned as early as v. 3 and further references occur in vv. 27, 73, 78, 83 and 85, and silver (vv. 73, 78 and 83) and money (*deners*, vv. 27 and 84) are also referred to. We are told that the pilgrims will take with them seven hundred camels, carrying enough gold and silver to last for seven years (vv. 73-74) and that the tents they have with them are made of white silk (v. 85). Signs of poverty and humility are conspicuously lacking, so this is not a standard pilgrimage. Later in the narrative both the patriarch (vv. 222-23) and King Hugo (vv. 839-40) will offer the Franks a portion of their treasure. Gifts, offerings in church and personal possessions are symbolic of wealth and power as well as of generosity. Charles will reject King Hugo's offer because he can provide his men with more wealth than they can manage to transport (vv. 842-43). Wealth and power always go hand in hand, but, as Vance notes (p. 173), in the mid-twelfth century social relationships were being 'monetarized'. Money was now a rival for the sword as a symbol of power as, even in the world of Saint-Denis, objects and services were being quantified in monetary terms.

Another significant element in the Introduction is the motif of heads (vv. 2, 10, 16, 20, 25, 41 and 42). Heads can wear crowns, which symbolize royal power (vv. 2, 6, 10, 15-16, 20). In ceremonial contexts, the combination of head and crown creates the effect of superiority which monarchs seek to convey. Charles sees the relationship between the act of placing the crown on his head and the public image this creates as central to his power and prestige (vv. 9-10) and it is this association which is targeted by the queen (vv. 15-16). Indeed, an interesting aspect of the *Pèlerinage* is that the entire plot is set in motion by the union between a king's head and a man-made object placed upon it. But heads can also be cut off by way of punishment, and this is what will happen to the queen, says Charles, if she has lied (vv. 24-25, 42, 55). Because she has doubted his power, her head will be removed by the king's own sword, the very instrument which is symbolic of his power in action (v. 25). In this case the sword will become an instrument of revenge.[4]

What conclusions can we draw from a study of the Introduction? Is the text so far entirely serious in intent, or are there already signs of a desire on the part of the author to amuse his audience? If at least part of the essence of the comic is to exploit the gap between reality and ideal, then the way in which the queen brings her husband down to earth is certainly comic. The fact that in this family quarrel the husband is both a great emperor and a famous epic hero can only add to the humour. Moreover, the way in which the queen retracts so swiftly, and her desperate claim that she was only joking and cannot even remember the foreign king's name, can be interpreted as amusing. But the feeling remains that the opening lines of this text are predominantly serious. Charles's anger and the threatened decapitation are chilling enough and there is nothing amusing about the queen's willingness to risk her life by way of exculpation by ordeal (one notes here the legal vocabulary: *s'escundirai, jurer serement, porter juise, par creance, s'estordre*, vv. 34-37, 43). Her offer to jump from the highest tower in Paris (v. 36) introduces a motif which will be encountered again in the context of Charles's victory over King Hugo (vv. 560-61, 779). Gosman makes a convincing case for viewing the text in terms of the legitimation of Capetian principles. At stake in the opening lines would be the link between the crown as symbol of both the royal persona (*corona regis*) and the Frankish kingdom as institution (*corona regni*). To doubt Charles is to doubt the political principles he embodies.

(ii) The Visit to Jerusalem (vv. 98-238)

Some of the details relating to Charles's actual journey to Jerusalem have puzzled

---

[4] Medieval French has two words for head, *chef* and *teste*, and we note that here the queen has a *teste* (v. 25, 55) whereas Charles has a *chef* (vv. 2, 10, 20, 41), the term which is often regarded as the more distinguished of the two. Like the Charles of the *Chanson de Roland* (v. 799), Charles swears by his head ('par mun chef', v. 41). See also vv. 489, 632, 647 and 742, and P. Le Gentil, '*Teste* et *chef* dans *la Chanson de Roland*', *Romania*, 71 (1950), 49-65.

scholars (see note to vv. 100-08). Whatever the precise route taken, however, the author clearly wants the audience to have enough information to permit them to imagine the journey being undertaken. He mentions the locations visited (Burgundy, Bavaria, Greece, etc.), the peoples encountered (Turks, Persians and a hated race) and the terrain negotiated (a great stretch of water, forests, mountains). The journey passes without incident and it prefaces a sojourn in Jerusalem which can only be described as delightful and successful, if perhaps ultimately, at least for Charles's men, a little tedious. From their arrival on a fine, bright day (v. 109) to their departure under the escort of the patriarch of Jerusalem himself (vv. 244-54), the Franks benefit from the admiration heaped on Charles and they enjoy a high level of hospitality. The quality of the hospitality is symbolized by the speed with which their needs are catered for (v. 247). Similar alacrity will also be manifested in Constantinople (vv. 703, 833).

Though the visit to Jerusalem begins well, it could have opened disastrously, had the patriarch taken exception to the behaviour of Charles and his men when they entered a church and sat in the seats once used by Christ and the apostles (vv. 116-22). Once more the issue here is one of power and authority. Disconcertingly, the patriarch points out that no one had ever dared to enter the church without his permission (vv. 149-50). Charles not only enters, but goes as far as to sit on a chair which was sealed off by some form of enclosure (v. 117) and therefore presumably out of bounds. Charles also allows his men to sit on the other twelve seats. Does such behaviour betoken his conviction that he enjoys the necessary authority for such acts, which were certainly fraught with risk? Or should we see his behaviour as evidence of crass ignorance or overweening pride? Fortunately, Charles is not criticized for what he has done and his authority is actually confirmed by the patriarch. Thus his status is curiously enhanced, not undermined, by his action.

In this scene the poet again makes use of the element of surprise. Whereas one might have expected the Franks to exhibit a degree of discretion with regard to these particular seats (in vv. 115-18 the poet has already made the audience aware of whose seats they were), they immediately sit down on them. There is surely a comic element here: 'Fools rush in where angels fear to tread.' But from the political point of view, the Charles of Saint-Denis, convinced that as monarch he enjoys divine support, demonstrates in this Jerusalem church the courage of his convictions. Not only does he get away with what he has done, but he even appears to receive from the patriarch the significant title of Charles Maines (Charlemagne), crowned above all kings (v. 158).[5] This ecclesiastical accolade is a boost to Charles's ego, and the fact that the poet associates him and his men with Christ and the apostles, here and elsewhere, cannot be coincidental. Charles's link with God affords him a quite remarkable degree of independence from outside interference, be it temporal or spiritual. If God loves him (cf. v. 796), he has little to fear from others. Of course, the higher he climbs towards God, the harder he falls if anything goes wrong! The poet may be preparing him and the audience for the catastrophe to come.

The Jerusalem episode can be divided into three parts: (a) the section which precedes the first mention of the relics (vv. 98-159), (b) the discussion of the relics and the proof of their efficacy (vv. 160-203), and (c) the description of other aspects of the four months which the Franks spend there (vv. 204-38). In vv. 116-17 we should note the allusion first to twelve seats and then to a thirteenth, which has been sealed off. The importance of the numbers twelve and thirteen is reinforced by Charles's remark to the patriarch that he has already overcome twelve kings and is looking for a thirteenth (vv. 152-53). This statement recalls both his boast to his wife that he will conquer yet more cities (v. 11) and his second reason for leaving France, to visit a king of whom he has heard tell (v. 72).[6] Will this king become his thirteenth victim? We should also note that in this scene in Jerusalem Charles's attention is drawn to the architecture and the beauty of the church which the Franks enter (vv. 113-14, 133-27). The quality of the building lends dignity and prestige to what transpires within it. Moreover, just as Charles is impressed by the great beauty of the church (v. 123), so a Jew, who enters the church, is impressed by Charles's own appearance, in particular by his fierce countenance (vv. 129-31).[7] So great is the power which emanates from Charles

---

[5] In the manuscript, which reads 'Aies nun Charles sur tuz reis curunez', the term *Maines* has probably been omitted by error. The forms *Carlemaines / Karlemaines* appear only after v. 158 (see note to this line). But even the designation 'sur tuz reis curunez' is sufficient to designate the special position which the patriarch is attributing to Charles.

[6] One notes the linguistic similarity between v. 72 ('E irrai un rei requerre dount ai oi parler') and v. 153 ('Li trezime vois querre dunt ai oi parler').

[7] Charles' fierce countenance is known to us from the *Chanson de Roland* (vv. 118, 142, etc.).

that the Jew rushes to the patriarch to ask for baptism (vv. 129-39). It is presumably because of his relative independence and impartiality as a witness that the Jew has been chosen for the function of stating that Charles and his men are Christ and the apostles (vv. 139-40). Such a pronouncement is calculated to galvanize any churchman into action and the patriarch duly gathers his priests together. In their finery, they proceed in splendid procession towards the church (vv. 141-44), prefiguring the future occasion when Charles himself will process in the company of King Hugo of Constantinople (vv. 808-10, 821).

If all this, especially the view that Charles is a new Christ, seems distinctly serious in tone, commentators have not failed to notice that in many ways Charles behaves like an innocent abroad. Aebischer thought that he should be regarded as 'un vulgaire touriste, ou mieux comme un touriste vulgaire' ('Sur Quelques Passages', p. 821). It is by no means impossible to see Charles's behaviour as comically inappropriate and to envisage the patriarch as failing, unlike the queen, to administer the dressing-down he deserves. From this perspective, the reaction of the Jew would represent a farcical misreading of the situation. The title of Charles Maines would thus be unmerited and its bestowal would merely be a postponement of something which is inevitable, the time when he will be cut down to size.

The second section of the Jerusalem episode is taken up by the account of the relics, which, in so far as they constitute a link between the visits to Jerusalem and to Constantinople, are of considerable importance to the structure of the text. They are important both within each episode and during the transition from the one to the other. Introduced into the text in a somewhat abrupt fashion, they occupy three laisses (IX-XI) and take up a large proportion of the space (around one third) devoted to the Jerusalem episode. Immediately after receiving the name Charlemagne, the Emperor of the Franks says: 'Give me, if you please, some of your holy relics, which I shall take back to France, for I wish the country to be illuminated by them' (vv. 160-61). The patriarch's response to this startlingly brusque request is surprisingly positive, or certainly surprising in its generosity: 'You will have them in abundance' (v. 162). He then enumerates the relics which he intends to bestow on Charles: (1) The arm of St Simeon, (2) The head of St Lazarus, (3) The blood of St Stephen, (4) The shroud of Jesus, (5) The nail from Jesus's foot, (6) The crown from Jesus's head, (7) The chalice which he blessed, (8) A silver bowl, (9) A knife, (10) Hair from St

Peter's beard and from his head, (11) Some of Mary's milk, (12) Mary's holy shift.

In a poem in which numbers, especially twelve and thirteen, are important, we can note that relic number 10 (St Peter's hair) could be divided into two. Such hair-splitting would give us a total of thirteen rather than twelve relics. An examination of the list shows that three items relate to the Last Supper (7-9), four or five to saints (1-3, 10) and two to the Virgin Mary (11-12), whose milk was indeed still venerated as a relic in the twelfth century. The relics are said by the patriarch to be the finest on earth (v. 169) and he predicts that they will perform great miracles ('grant vertuz', v. 186). The appearance of the term *vertu(z)* 'power, miracle' is noteworthy in view of its earlier presence in a significant passage (v. 56). The poet soon repeats the notion that the relics possess great power (v. 192) and points out that their efficacy is immediately in evidence. A cripple, who has not moved for seven years, walks again and is restored to full health (vv. 193-95). The power exhibited by the relics is no doubt introduced at this point because they will later be required to act to the advantage of the Franks at a critical point in the text. The patriarch is sufficiently impressed by this miracle to have bells tolled throughout the city (vv. 196-97).

The second scene in which the power of the relics is significant is the journey to Constantinople. In v. 255 the poet repeats his remark concerning their power (cf. v. 192), and on this occasion the waters part whenever the Franks draw near to a ford and sight is restored to every blind person whom they encounter. Once more the lame are said to walk again and, in addition, the dumb begin to speak (vv. 256-58). Although their role at this stage of the narrative is somewhat marginal, the relics clearly have a part to play in the restoration of health and in the resolution of any difficulties which the Franks might experience as they progress towards their desired goal. It could be said that in this second role the relics take the place of weapons. However, their success is so stunning and instantaneous that their very credibility may be compromised. For Brians, for example, the relics are being ridiculed and therefore they cannot be taken seriously (p. 164). We shall return to this issue shortly.

At this point it may be useful to look ahead to later stages of the narrative. The early success of the relics prefigures their importance when the lives of the Franks are threatened as a result of their jests. Charlemagne will order the relics to be brought before him and in their presence the Franks will pray for God's help in protecting them from King Hugo's threatened revenge (vv. 667-71). Most critics agree that it is thanks to the power of the relics that God intervenes. Again the relics act as a substitute for weaponry, as the Franks would surely have had recourse to their swords to assist them in such an emergency. Thus the relics are instrumental in creating the peaceful victory to which Charles alludes in vv. 858-59, and they succeed in becoming a means of conquest. Moreover, the relics even have an important role to play in the conclusion. On his return to France, Charlemagne enters the church of Saint-Denis, and after prostrating himself in prayer he places the nail and the crown on the altar (vv. 863-66). The other relics are distributed throughout the kingdom (v. 867). The question which arises (and I shall return to it later) is whether there is a link between the poem and Saint-Denis itself. It is by no means impossible that the presence of specific relics in Saint-Denis serves to explain, at least partially, the reason why the author constructed the story as he did. 'La *Chanson du Pèlerinage*', wrote Bédier, 'est essentiellement un récit de translation de reliques' (IV, p. 154).

There is an interesting comparison to be made between the relics in the *Pèlerinage* and those in the *Chanson de Roland*. In the latter poem, the pommel of Roland's sword Durendal is said to contain four relics: St Peter's tooth, St Basil's blood, some of St Denis's hair and part of the Virgin Mary's clothing (vv. 2346-48). In the *Pèlerinage*, Charles receives not St Peter's tooth but some of his beard and hair. St Basil's blood is replaced by the blood of the first Christian martyr, St Stephen. Mary's raiment, this time specifically her chemise, also occurs again and some of her milk is now added to the list of relics. This raises once more the question of whether the author was deliberately echoing elements in the *Chanson de Roland*. If so, was his intention to mock or to parody this poem and its characters? There is also a significant link between the relics in the *Pèlerinage* and those in a Latin text known as the *Descriptio*, which the author could have known and used. In this work, Charles obtains his relics in Constantinople, where they had been discovered and guarded by the Empress Helen. In the *Descriptio* the relics are the crown of thorns, a nail from the cross, the shroud, the Virgin Mary's *interula* 'chemise' and St Simeon's arm, corresponding respectively to items 6, 5, 12, 4 and 1 of the relics listed in the *Pèlerinage*. All three texts contain references to saints and to the Virgin's clothing. The *Pèlerinage* and the *Descriptio* mention items relating to Christ's Passion (the shroud, the nail and the crown of thorns) and the *Roland* and the *Pèlerinage* both mention hair. The *Pèlerinage* author, we note, shows a particular interest in items relating to food: the chalice, the silver plate, the knife and milk.

At the time when the *Pèlerinage* was composed, relics were important to Saint-Denis and indeed to churches and monasteries throughout France. At the end of the eleventh and the beginning of the twelfth century in particular, relics entered France in large numbers. There were three types of relics: the holy person's body or parts of it, objects relating closely to the holy person and objects which had touched the holy person's remains (such as oils from the tomb collected in *ampulae*). All the relics in the *Pèlerinage* fall into the first two categories. In the eyes of the Church, after relics of Christ himself or those of the Passion (nails from the crucifixion, thorns from the crown, pieces of the True Cross, etc.) came those relating to the Virgin Mary (the tunic she wore at Christ's birth, which by the ninth century was supposedly located at Chartres), her hair, her nail parings and her milk. Relics of the apostles and the saints came next and they constituted the largest category. Saints' relics were venerated well before the time of Charlemagne and, significantly, they were appealed to for miraculous cures. Charlemagne himself extended the role of relics by decreeing that all oaths had to be sworn on them. As in the *Pèlerinage* (vv. 198-201), reliquaries were made to house these remains, and ivory, gems, enamelwork and precious metals were used in their construction.[8]

Grisgby, having pointed out that the author no doubt knew that Saint-Denis had many relics, asks the question: 'Was he bragging about them or mocking them?' ('The Relics' Rôle', p. 34). There is nothing inherently comic about the relics taken individually. If we are going to tax the author with a lack of seriousness, we might wish to focus on the number involved. For one reason or another, the poet evidently felt a need to emphasise the importance of the relics, but did he need to cite twelve or thirteen of them? An element of comic exaggeration certainly cannot be ruled out here. Nor can such factors as the remarkable ease with which Charles obtains the relics, his forwardness in asking for them and the astonishing speed with which they cure the sick. They can even make the waters part at

---

[8] For a brief, but effective discussion of relics see the entry 'Relics and Reliquaries' by Paula L. Gerson in *Medieval France: An Encyclopedia* (New York and London: Garland, 1995), pp. 790-93.

fords (v. 256), the very sections of rivers which should not have caused the Franks much of a problem in the first place. Just how a contemporary audience would have regarded such descriptions is hard to judge. One suspects that they must have raised at least a smile, but this does not mean that the author was mocking the relics, either those in his poem or those at Saint-Denis. His primary purpose would have been to call attention to the literary function of the relics within the narrative and he would have relied on his audience's ability to bear their efficacy in mind when their use became critical to the survival of the Franks.[9]

The third and last section of this episode describes the Franks' peaceful sojourn in Jerusalem. Thanks to Charles's extreme wealth, the Franks enjoy a life of splendour (v. 206) and they found a church called the Latanie, which, we are told, continues to attract speakers of diverse tongues (*li language*, v. 209). It had also become a market-place for the sale of precious cloth and numerous spices (vv. 210-12). In his description of the churches in Jerusalem, the poet was clearly drawing on travellers' tales and perhaps on written descriptions of them and in fact he amalgamates several churches (see notes to vv. 114 and 208-09). In a form of intervention which has no equivalent elsewhere in the text, the poet asserts that God is still in his heaven and will bring the merchants to justice (v. 213). He either took, or wanted his audience to think that he took, a hard line on mercantile activities on ecclesiastical property. He also must have wanted his audience to think that he knew the facts about Charles's foundation in Jerusalem and decided that such information was useful to his purpose. The author also decided to have the patriarch, even after all his hospitality and the gift of priceless relics, behave yet more munificently by refusing Charles's offer of a hundred mules laden with gold and silver and stating that the Franks were at liberty to take from his treasure as much as they could carry (vv. 220-23).

The poet also has the patriarch give the Franks a surprising warning and make an important request of them. He tells them to be careful of the Saracens and pagans, who are threatening Christianity, and he even asks the Franks to make an effort to destroy them (vv. 224-27). By so doing, he introduces an unexpected note of danger into the contented world of Jerusalem, danger both to the Franks and to the Christian faith itself. Although the

---

[9] Horrent stresses the reality of the relics for the contemporary public and their essentially serious treatment (*Le Pèlerinage de Charlemagne: essai d'explication littéraire*, pp. 39-45). See also Morf, pp. 224-29.

patriarch does not specify precisely where these Saracens and pagans are to be found (one might have assumed that he was referring specifically to a potential threat to the Franks as they journeyed towards Constantinople), Charles replies by saying that he will go to Spain without delay (vv. 229-30). The poet adds that he kept his word and that, as a result, Roland and the twelve peers met their deaths (vv. 231-32). Was the poet's intention here to create a clear link between his poem and the *Chanson de Roland*, or at least to allude to the tradition of Roland's death in Spain? By this allusion to Charles's campaign in Spain, he certainly forges an association with a world, both literary and historical, outside the text and thereby offers his audience the opportunity to compare the characters in his story with those in other traditions. It is therefore legitimate to ask whether Charles has so far behaved in a way which is befitting for the great emperor of history and legend. How do he and his men compare with the famous peers who, in a text such as the *Chanson de Roland*, sacrificed themselves for their lord and for the Christian faith? The poet surely intended his audience to ask these questions. The non-military activities of the Franks in Jerusalem can be contrasted with the frequently tragic universe of epic poems and even with the precarious world in which members of the audience would have lived. But as they make their way to Constantinople, life for the Franks remains tranquil and they encounter no hostility or obstacles.

What conclusions can we draw from the Jerusalem episode? First, that the text is not shaping up to become a comic masterpiece. There are certainly comic elements in evidence and we are undoubtedly not dealing with a typical *chanson de geste*. The Franks have been presented so far as a happy and successful band of pilgrims. Jerusalem is in some ways an extension of the world from which they came, but here, paradoxically, Charles receives the treatment he had expected in his own country. The patriarch's apparent bestowal on him of the name Charlemagne contrasts markedly with the queen's refusal to endorse his image of superiority. Here we have a clear comic contrast. But what the poet has done is to set up a contrast with the past and at the same time prepare for a further contrast to come. The joy with which the Franks depart from Jerusalem is at the opposite pole from the despair into which they will sink during their visit to Constantinople.

(iii) The Visit to Constantinople (vv. 239-857)

Like the journey to Jerusalem, the journey to Constantinople, begun in the company of the patriarch and punctuated by successful performances from the relics, passes peacefully. Details of the itinerary are briefer on this occasion but no less puzzling (see note to vv. 260-61). As in the case of Jerusalem, first impressions of Constantinople, its architecture, trees and flowers, are very positive (vv. 263-66). Gone are the Jew, the patriarch and the clerics, to be replaced by a vast number of knights and comely maidens, clad in garments of silk and disporting themselves in great delight (vv. 267-74). Even more impressive is King Hugo himself, who is found not in his palace but, surprisingly and incongruously, at his golden plough. Gold and silver are in evidence again (vv. 284, 288, 291, 295), and sitting on a magnificent silk cushion, with grey silk draping down from four posts which surround him (vv. 289-94), the Emperor of Greece and Constantinople can immediately be seen as a potential threat to Charles's supremacy. We have already a firm impression of remarkable ingenuity and fabulous wealth. Had King Hugo the Strong been a disappointing or run-of-the mill monarch, the story could have quickly lost its edge. Politically speaking, Hugo is a threat not only to Charles but also to the entire feudal system, based as it is on the distinction between members of three distinct orders, those who work, those who fight and those who pray (*laboratores, bellatores* and *oratores*).[10]

The first meeting between Charles and Hugo is cordial and promising. King Hugo heaps compliments and offers of hospitality on Charles in a way which is reminiscent of the behaviour of the patriarch of Jerusalem (vv. 310-16).[11] The inferiority of Frankish civilisation is highlighted by Charles's amazement when Hugo leaves his golden plough unattended and apparently exposed to theft. Charles is told firmly that theft is completely unknown in Hugo's territory (vv. 320-35). William of Orange makes matters worse by

[10] See Georges Duby, *Les trois Ordres ou l'imaginaire du féodalisme* (Paris: Gallimard, 1978), trans. A. Goldhammer as *The Three Orders: Feudal Society Imagined* (Chicago and London: University of Chicago Press, 1980). For a discussion of Hugo's plough, see Polak, pp. 159-62. Polak regards King Hugo as the first of the marvels of Constantinople (p. 159).

[11] An odd note is struck by the poet's description of Charles, as seen through the eyes of King Hugo. Charles has a fierce look on his face, large and solid arms and a slim and delicate body (vv. 303-04). This is not perhaps the description one associates with a great warrior king and it may be that Charles is here the butt of the poet's humour.

stating that, if the plough were in France, he and Bertrand would soon have destroyed it with picks and hammers (vv. 326-28). Cracks are beginning to show in the Frankish value system and in the composure of Charles's men. Surprise is becoming the order of the day.

King Hugo's palace is characterised by its abundance of ermine-clad knights and by its magnificent furnishings, paintings and marble columns. Twice the author uses the expression 'richesce grant' (vv. 342, 362) and a marked contrast is set up between the level of material wealth in the respective kingdoms. Charles himself is already cognizant of the gulf which separates his own possessions from those of his host. Particularly remarkable within the palace is a life-like sculpture of two children carrying horns of white ivory in their mouths. Moreover, the whole palace will revolve, we are told, if it is struck by a wind blowing from the sea, and the children's horns will blare forth like the sound of thunder or the tolling of a huge bell (vv. 352-61). Clearly, Constantinople and its wonders are a cut above anything the Franks have experienced hitherto. They are in another world, almost the Other World. Even at this early stage of their visit, any lingering sense of superiority they might be nurturing is being thoroughly tested.

Charles is unstinting in his praise of Hugo's palace and he compares it favourably to those owned by some of the great names of antiquity. References to Alexander and Constantine come as no surprise, but the mention of Crescentius of Rome is more unusual. The principal allusion here seems to be to the Castel S. Angelo in Rome, originally Hadrian's Mausoleum, which was held by Crescentius against Otto III at the end of the tenth century. This building was known for some remarkable features and it may have been the closest the poet could come to the sort of building he was describing in Constantinople.[12] It is to the special effects of Hugo's palace that the poet now has recourse, in order to rid the Franks of any remaining sense of dignity and control. To have the Franks move from the visual shock of realising their financial inferiority to the physical shock of being sent tumbling to the ground is a masterstroke. The Franks have become truly comic figures, floundering in a world which begins by astounding them and then literally floors them.

---

[12] See my article '"Ne n'out Crisans de Rome, qui tanz honurs bastid"'.

The occasion for this lesson is the great storm which strikes the palace and sets it in motion, making it revolve like a windmill. Inside, the tranquil conditions resemble those of paradise, with the statues of the children blowing their horns and smiling at each other. Outside is a violent storm. Unable to cope with this new experience, Charles sits down; his men are thrown to the ground, where they lie with their heads covered, bemoaning their fate (vv. 368-91). Things are now looking very bad for the visitors, whose stay in Constantinople has swiftly degenerated to the level of farce. If Charles is to salvage anything from this attempt to prove his superiority over King Hugo, he and his men need a speedy boost to their morale. The great warriors found in the *Chanson de Roland* and other poems are indeed in a sorry plight. They are faced with a king who has even managed the momentous task of controlling the elements and harnessing their power to bolster his own prestige.

A temporary boost for the Franks is provided in the form of the ending of the storm and the provision of a good dinner, at which the wine flows and the entertainment is of high quality (vv. 398-414). Oliver is further cheered when he sets eyes on the emperor's beautiful daughter. But the audience is not reassured with regard to the standard of Frankish behaviour when he mutters that, if she were in France, he would have his way with her (vv. 404-07). There is a comic element here. To an audience which was no doubt aware of the wise and courtly hero of the *Chanson de Roland*, Oliver's sexual ambitions must have appeared more than a little incongruous. His remark is certainly one of the elements in the text which would have raised a laugh from the audience. It also paves the way for his more significant impact on the text in later scenes.

The twelve beds in King Hugo's chamber, with a thirteenth in the centre, cannot but be reminiscent of the seats in the Jerusalem church (vv. 425-26, cf. vv. 116-17). The beds are of superb quality, a characteristic of Hugo's other possessions. The king is naturally keen to discover whether his new visitors will make good long-term guests, and being of cunning disposition (v. 438) he adopts the ploy of placing a spy in a convenient hiding-place. From his point of view, this ploy ultimately backfires, but without the spy the story could not have proceeded as it does. The question is: will the Franks conduct themselves in seemly fashion? All would have been well if they had yielded to the pressures of a disturbing day and retired to bed immediately. Instead, they succumb to Hugo's additional supply of wine

(v. 437) and to the Frankish convention of late-night jesting. These boastful jests (*gabs*) take the form of an exaggerated claim to be able to perform seemingly impossible acts, aimed at entertaining and astounding the onlookers. The *gabs* assume in this poem an importance which is analogous to, but even greater than, that of the relics.

Thirteen of the Franks jest, including Charles himself, who is both the instigator and the inaugurator of the series. The ritualistic aspect of the boasting ceremony is reflected in the formulaic language used to describe it. After he starts the ball rolling (v. 453), Charles himself makes the request to eight of the twelve peers, on each occasion using the verb *gaber* together with the name of the peer in question. It is Roland, however, who asks Oliver to jest (v. 484) and also, apparently, Roland who asks Archbishop Turpin (v. 493). William of Orange volunteers himself (v. 507) and Bertram introduces his uncle, Ernalz de Girunde (v. 566). Ten of the eleven peers asked to jest reply by using the adverb *volenteres* (the exception is Turpin, v. 494). Eight of the peers respond by saying that they will jest in accordance with Charles's command (vv. 470, 494, 541, 554, 580), permission (vv. 485, 520) or pleasure (v. 592). The framing device is completed by the intervention of the spy who, with one exception (v. 576), prefaces each of his responses with the exclamation 'Par Deu' (vv. 465, 482, 490, 505, 515, 528, 538, 551, 562, 589, 600, 616).

The spy's reaction to the *gabs* is in some cases positive, in others negative. He can be impressed by a good jest (vv. 505, 576) and by the strength (vv. 465, 539) or the toughness of the jester (vv. 539, 553, 577, 578). Alternatively, he can condemn a bad jest (vv. 482, 600) and claim that it will bring shame on King Hugo (v. 491). His interest in the concept of shame is conveyed by way he comments on two occasions that the *gab* in question will not in fact cause the king any shame (vv. 506, 617). Indeed, it is with the term *huntage* that the poet concludes the series of jests (v. 617), at which point the Franks fall asleep. A repeated reaction of the spy is to comment on King Hugo's foolishness (vv. 466, 467, 483, 530, 563, 590) in giving lodgings to the Franks. In so doing, he is, of course, reintroducing the theme of folly, which appeared in the text as early as the first laisse. Whether or not he is impressed by the *gab*, the spy also likes to suggest that the Franks are mad (vv. 528, 551, 562, 589). He also plants in the mind of the audience the possibility that, as a result of the *gabs*, the Franks may be sent packing (vv. 468, 564). Even worse, before the sequence of *gabs* is over, the spy has hinted at the possibility that the Franks may be called upon to put them into practice (vv. 529, 578, 616).[13]

Charlemagne's jest, in which he claims to be able to cleave through two hauberks and two helmets studded with gems and plant his sword deeply into the ground, is to an extent reminiscent of his victorious blow in the *Chanson de Roland*, in which he breaks Baligant's helmet, also studded with gems, and slices through his head (vv. 3615-19). Roland's imagined exploit with his olifant must derive from his close association with the horn in the same epic. Although Oliver's sexual heroics are a far cry from his status as Roland's wise and trusty companion-in-arms, they can be viewed against the background of his important function within that poem. Oliver's jest possesses a delightful incongruity, and coming after two typical epic boasts, it gains maximum comic impact from its contrast with them and with Oliver's known behaviour. Some of the *gabs* also recall Biblical scenes. Roland's confidence that the wind generated by his olifant will cause the gates of Constantinople to come crashing together may have reminded the audience of the collapse of the walls of Jericho (Joshua 6. 20). Ogier's destruction of the palace by pulling down its supporting pillar recalls the destruction of the Temple by Samson (Judges 16. 26-30). Bernard's flood has clear links with the Biblical Flood (Genesis 6-8) and perhaps also with the crossing of the Red Sea (Exodus 14. 21-30).[14]

The reactions of the spy demonstrate that the *gabs* fall into two categories: those which glorify the individual's achievements for their own sake and those which target King Hugo or his property. There are six *gabs*, which resemble circus acts or stunts, in the first category, and seven in the second. But what explanation can we give for the Franks' boastful jests and for the nature of the *gabs* themselves? First, as far as the Franks themselves are concerned, the act of *gaber* is by no means unusual. When reprimanded by King Hugo, Charles refers to the Frankish custom of indulging in playful banter on retiring to bed: 'Si

---

[13] The repetitive nature of the spy's language, which is largely formulaic, is certainly a comic feature of the poem. Some of the spy's expressions are even repeated by King Hugo. See Cobby, *Ambivalent Conventions*, pp. 91-97.

[14] For discussion and further examples of Biblical and hagiographical parallels in the *gabs* see Cobby, 'Religious Elements', pp. 368-71, and *Ambivalent Conventions*, pp. 143-45.

est tel custume en France, a Paris e a Cartres, / Quant Franceis sunt culchiez, que si giuent e gabent' (vv. 654-55). It is important to note that the verb *gaber* is coupled here with the verb *giuer* 'to play'. For Charles there is nothing inherently serious about the act of *gaber*. For him it is associated with frivolity and entertainment rather than with any genuine claim to the possession of superior skills. It is for this reason that I prefer the term 'jest' to 'boast' when a single word is required to designate the *gabs*. This does not mean that the *gabs*, which are the comic expression of militaristic pride, do not contain a strong element of boasting. It merely indicates that for Charles, spokesman for his men, the words uttered in these circumstances were not stimulated by any genuine desire to offend. He also acknowledges that they were a blend of the wise and the foolish (v. 656). Charles lays the blame for this particular session of jesting squarely on the quantity of wine offered to the Franks by King Hugo (vv. 650, 653, 665, 685) and he clearly sees drunkenness (vv. 650, 685) as an excuse for what took place in the bed-chamber.

Charles also has a complaint of his own to make. He sees the action of leaving a spy in the chamber as reprehensible (v. 686). He refers to a second Frankish *custume*, whereby such an action would have been considered a crime against the feudal bond itself (vv. 688-89). Such was the importance of custom to contemporary French society that the poet is using Charles's accusation to highlight a fundamental difference between the two cultures. However, Charles's attempt to transfer the blame on to King Hugo fails, because where Charles sees playfulness Hugo sees a serious crime against that key concept of feudal society: loyalty. His first questions to the spy are: 'What are they doing? Will they remain faithful to me?' (vv. 623-24).[15] This enquiry recalls the question put by Charles to his wife in the opening lines of the text. He too expected loyalty from her. The accusation of *folie* which Hugo levels against the Franks (v. 629) also reminds one of the scene at Saint-Denis, as does his designated punishment, the loss of their heads (vv. 633, 647). Hugo intends to teach Charles a lesson (v. 660), and Charles is now getting a taste of his own medicine. For Hugo interprets the act of *gaber* as hostile, just as Charles had earlier interpreted his wife's remark in similar fashion. Hugo further taxes Charles with displaying great recklessness (vv. 630,

---

[15] The precise interpretation of v. 624 is not certain. See the note to this line.

645) and derision (v. 643). When Hugo says 'Nel dusez ja penser par si grant legerie' (v. 645), we are reminded of Charles's observation to the queen: 'Nel dusés ja penser, dame, de ma vertuz' (v. 56). Ironically, Hugo's overall sense of outrage is reminiscent of Charles's view of the queen's insulting comparison between himself and this very king.

What support can we find for Hugo's view of the *gabs*? Can it be said that they were deliberately intended to mock and deride Hugo and his men and that they were indeed the product of folly and great recklessness? It may be useful to note that the *gabs* fit not only into a context of playfulness and seriousness but also into one of knightly activity and passivity on the part of the Franks. For, in spite of their status as pilgrims, the Franks are, both within the epic tradition and this particular poem, fundamentally warriors. They are described here as *chevalers* (v. 781) and *barons* (*barun*, vv. 241, 246, 781, *barnét / barnez*, vv. 254, 400, 821, 829, *barnage*, v. 312). They are frequently designated as a hardy and fierce band of men (vv. 98, 111, 639, 649). Adjectives used to qualify them are *adurez* 'tough, hardy' (vv. 62, 65), *fer* 'fierce' (vv. 111, 639, 629) and *ruiste* 'mighty, strong' (vv. 254, 400, 657). When the Franks take up their scrips and their staffs, it is implied that their normal equipment consists of lance, shield and sharp sword (v. 79). The patriarch confirms their chivalric credentials, for he evidently views them as being capable of destroying the Saracens (v. 227). Charles stresses to the patriarch that he has already conquered twelve kings and that he is intent on defeating a thirteenth (vv. 152-53), and King Hugo claims to have heard that no king on earth had such great warriors (v. 312). Even though no fighting takes place, there are two references in the text to a possible pitched battle (vv. 452, 859).

The possession of fundamental chivalric and physical skills must lie behind the *gabs* in the form in which we have them. These warriors, armed only with the equipment of the pilgrim, were taken by Charles to Jerusalem, where they spent some time in easy enjoyment of the amenities on offer. There they accomplished little more than the foundation of a church, which has, as Burrell observes (p. 50), been turned into a combination of a grocery store and a haberdashery (vv. 207-13). It would not be surprising if these men were suffering from a degree of frustration at not being able to put into practice the military skills which had been the basis of their way of life before leaving France. The *gabs*, from this point of view, are engendered by an innate wish to demonstrate their physical skills. The concomitant desire to maximise their self-esteem is analogous to the way in which Charles had sought confirmation of his image in the opening lines of the poem. It is no surprise, then, that the Franks aim in their *gabs* to impress the imagined audience with their strength, skill and ability to manipulate various pieces of equipment, which, of course, have to be borrowed from their hosts. In the course of the *gabs*, we find references to swords (vv. 458, 542, 546, 547, 636), lances (v. 604), hauberks (vv. 456, 460, 533, 536), helmets (vv. 459, 460) and shields (v. 593). With them the Franks will perform remarkable acts, of a type which would be beyond the capabilities of their hosts. By impressing King Hugo and his men with their presumed physical skills, the Franks go some way towards redressing, at least in their own eyes, the balance of power and towards gaining revenge for the sense of inferiority, humiliation and even fear which they had suffered as a consequence of the revolving palace (vv. 385-91).

There can also be little doubt that the Franks are motivated by envy. They had stared in wonder at a good many things in the city of Constantinople. The very sight of the city with its roofs topped with eagles, its shimmering bridges and its magnificent orchards was awe-inspiring (vv. 262-66). Then there was King Hugo's golden plough, his canopy of silk, his cushion, his stool and his golden sceptre (vv. 281-95). All this was as nothing in comparison to his palace and hall, bedecked with silks. Even the wealthy Charles himself reacted to all this magnificence by scorning his own possessions, and the Franks preface their *gabs* with a wish that Charles could have purchased the palace or won it in battle (vv. 448-52). The *gabs* can thus be interpreted as betraying a desire to dominate Hugo, to shame him by destroying his most precious possessions, his daughter, his palace and his self-esteem. The military and the political implications of the *gabs* come to the fore when Hugo backs down and decides not to maintain his original desire to see all the jests accomplished. He expresses his willingness to become Charles's vassal (v. 797) and Charles, we are told, is delighted that he has 'conquered' King Hugo without having had to fight him on the battlefield (vv. 858-59). Before the series of *gabs* begins, it would have appeared to the audience, and no doubt to the Franks themselves, that they were disconcertingly inadequate and the product of an inferior culture and values. The *gabs* are therefore a mental re-ordering of things, a verbal restoration of superiority, an indication that they were men to be reckoned with. The fact that the *gabs* do indeed lead to a new order, in which the Franks are shown to be superior to the Greeks, is a delicious irony of the text.

Faced with the threat to their lives, in the form of the loss of their heads, the Franks have the relics brought forward and they pray to God for salvation (vv. 668-70). As they are repeatedly presented to us as a vehicle for God's *vertut* (vv. 192, 196, 255), it would be natural to assume that the relics possess the power to summon up God's aid in an emergency. When he arrives, the angel shows that he shares the Greeks' distaste for the act of *gaber* and for the *folie* which the Franks have committed. The message he brings is that none of the *gabs* will fail, but also that the Franks must never again mock their fellow men (vv. 675-76). The angel does not say that God will take on all the *gabs* single-handedly, only that they will not fail, i.e. that God will support the Franks when they need support. He also does not rule out all forms of jesting, only *gabs* which are directed at other people (v. 675).

Knowing that the Franks must now accomplish their feats as stated, the audience has to ask the question: which *gab* will the king choose first? Then, when we know the first three choices, a further question arises: why does Hugo choose Oliver, William and Bernard to perform their *gabs*? The poet presumably wishes to have no more than three *gabs* performed, to avoid an excessively lengthy conclusion to his text. The chosen *gabs* must be effective in bringing Hugo rapidly to the point at which he is willing to capitulate. The six harmless *gabs* are therefore ruled out, as an account of their accomplishment would have been repetitive and, moreover, their successful execution would not have troubled Hugo to any great extent. Ogier's demolition of the central pillar would have killed all the occupants of the palace in the process (vv. 521-27). Like the angel, Hugo is sensitive to the concepts of *huntage* (v. 659), *folie* (v. 693) and *felonie* (v. 695), so it is natural for him to choose the first *gab* which elicited one of these responses from his spy: 'Grant huntage avez dit', comments the spy, on hearing Oliver's jest (v. 491). Once evening arrives, Hugo's daughter is led into a chamber which is bedecked with silks and curtains. As his daughter's virginity is at stake in Oliver's *gab*, one wonders whether we are meant to assume that anger has clouded Hugo's judgement. Such unthinkable behaviour could be seen as undermining his credibility and making him a less sympathetic figure in the eyes of the audience. Powerful lords in the audience would have shuddered at the idea of exposing their daughters to such an ordeal. A daughter was a valuable commodity and once deflowered her value would have been drastically reduced. Furthermore, the choice of Oliver is curious in that this *gab* cannot be verified by Hugo himself. Its verification requires the co-operation of his daughter. This, of course, offers the poet the advantage of permitting Oliver to get away with only the partial accomplishment of his jest. We also note that God seems not to be called upon to assist on this occasion.

Oliver's *gab* reintroduces to us the king's beautiful, wise and courtly daughter, whom Oliver had gazed upon during dinner. She is a potential heroine of a courtly romance and the role played by courtliness in this scene is important, as is the fact that, in spite of the grotesque nature of the circumstances, Oliver and the girl reach a compromise. The first couple to appear in this text, Charles and his queen, had conspicuously failed to so. In the event, both Oliver and the king's daughter emerge from the chamber with their dignity intact, and in true courtly fashion Oliver has acquired a beloved (*drue*, v. 724). The scene is in fact presented with great subtlety. Having entered the chamber in great fear, the girl breaks the ice by employing her courtliness to make what the author calls a noble statement (v. 710). She asks Oliver whether he left France with the intention of killing women. Oliver was no doubt not expecting such a disarming question, but one can imagine what his reply, both physically and verbally, could have been, had he been bent on accomplishing his *gab*. At best, the text would have been brought down to the level of an erotic fabliau. But Oliver too is courtly (v. 716) and he claims to have no wish to accomplish his desires with her (v. 719). This differs markedly from the aggressive view he expressed the first time he saw the king's daughter (v. 407). Something has intervened to cause him to look at things differently. Instead of raping her, he puts to her a possible compromise: she will become his sole beloved and acquit him with the king. Now trusting him, and being courtly, she accepts this offer (v. 725). So the author has used the concept of courtliness, mentioned three times (vv. 710, 716, 725), to enable the two participants in this scene to extract something positive from the potentially brutal consequences of the *gab* and the father's choice.

So it appears that the first *gab* has been accomplished without incurring the loss of the girl's virginity. The audience is therefore ill-prepared for v. 726, which tells us that Oliver 'did it to her no more than thirty times that night'. This line has caused a great deal of controversy (see note). Aebischer even refused to print it in view of its effect on Oliver's reputation. He sees Oliver's original *gab* as merely expressing a desire to kiss the girl a hundred times. Omission of the line could also be justified by the statement made by Koschwitz that the line was struck through in the manuscript, by the scribe or a later reviser. Unfortunately, this can no longer be verified. But even if at some stage it was struck out, the line at one time, however temporarily, had full status within the text, and Oliver certainly did express the desire to 'have' the girl a hundred times in a night (v. 488). Although it is not strictly necessary to the outcome of the scene, v. 726 corresponds to his wish to put a numerical figure on his sexual performance. The line is nothing if not shocking, and the desire to shock is, of course, a frequent comic device. In addition, even if reduced to more realistic proportions, there is still an element of epic exaggeration of a humorous type. Allied to the motif of courtliness, v. 726 helps the author to rescue the scene from its potential for brutality.

The king's anger is not diminished by the news he receives that Oliver has succeeded in his task. Making another logical choice, he then chooses William of Orange, whose threat to Hugo's property was the first *gab* to make the spy suggest that he should be forced to perform the stated act (vv. 508-16). The account of the execution of William's *gab*, unlike that of Oliver, which occupied thirty lines, is brief (vv. 744-52), and this time there is no room for doubt about its accomplishment to the letter. William duly demolishes some sixty feet of the palace wall with his *pelote* ('sphere'). It is interesting to note that, whereas no mention of God's intervention was made (or apparently needed) during Oliver's feat, we are now told that in William's case it was not his own strength but God's power which accomplished the task (v. 751). Thus the theme of power reappears in the text ('par Deu vertud', v. 751). The astonished Hugo puts William's success down, like that of Oliver, to the power of sorcery (vv. 733, 756). But he also reminds us of the serious political dimension to this poem when he makes the additional point that the Franks clearly intend to take over his territory and his property (v. 757).

If Hugo was tempted to relent after two successful *gabs*, his conviction that the stakes were as high as the loss of his kingdom would have made this difficult. To prove his point and confirm his superiority he only needs one failure on the part of the Franks. He now chooses not Ogier's *gab*, the next one to be designated as harmful by the spy and which would have caused the palace to collapse, but that proposed by Bernard, whom the spy classed as a madman (v. 562). The successful implementation of this *gab* must have seemed a very remote possibility, as it involved the deflection of the great river in the nearby valley so that it flowed through the city, soaking everyone in the process and causing Hugo himself to ascend the tallest tower in the city. In stating his choice, Hugo shows that he is not unmindful of the point made by Bernard (v. 561), that he himself would be able to come down from the tower only when Bernard gave him the order to do so (v. 770). He was therefore aware of the potential for total humiliation which this *gab* offered and he knew that its successful accomplishment could signify a transfer of power from the Greeks to the Franks.

For the Franks, the execution of Bernard's *gab* has its good and its bad side. It will be the one which secures victory for them over the Greeks, but it also causes them to take refuge, somewhat precariously, in an ancient pine tree (vv. 780-81). The author is certainly no respecter of reputations and this indignity is a sign that the comic spirit is certainly not absent from this poem. Far from appearing to be on the brink of victory, the Franks are forced to ask God to have pity on them (v. 782). Like its predecessor, the exploit itself is accomplished through God's help (v. 775), and when they hear Hugo admitting defeat in his tower the Franks pray to Jesus, whereupon God reverses his miracle: 'Deus i fist grant vertut pur amur Carlemaigne' (v. 791). This line is reminiscent of v. 2458 of the *Chanson de Roland*: 'Pur Karlemagne fist Deus vertuz mult granz.' But, whereas in the *Roland* God holds the sun stationary so that the Franks can enjoy more daylight in order to vanquish the Saracens, in the *Pèlerinage* he performs his miracle in order to extricate Charles and his men from the fix caused by their unnecessary and foolish jests. However, in both cases the miracle assists Charles in the winning of a victory.

The return of the river to its bed follows Hugo's undignified capitulation in the tower, where he is marooned. He offers Charles his treasure and his homage: he will hold his kingdom from him as a fief (vv. 785-87, 797). For all its comic overtones, this is a stunning victory. As the poet will later say, to win such a victory without a pitched battle is indeed a cause for rejoicing (vv. 858-59). For any contemporary monarch or feudal lord it is the stuff of dreams. Moreover, Charles has done what he set out to do: he has not only visited but also defeated a thirteenth king (cf. vv. 152-53). We note that, paradoxically, God's reversal of the effects of his miracle is preceded by an act of mercy on Charles's part (vv. 788-89), one which recalls both his failure to offer his wife a similar favour in the early stages of the text (v. 32) and Hugo's unwillingness to show his guests any sympathy or understanding. The poet himself intervenes to say that one should yield in the face of humility (v. 789), in other words show mercy where it is appropriate. Significantly, Charles's act of mercy prepares the closure of the text, just as his earlier refusal to pardon the queen and King Hugo's failure to show mercy to the Franks had shaped the structure of the text as we have it. King Hugo's flight up the tallest tower in the city, to avoid the swirling waters, also recalls the queen's willingness to throw herself down from the tallest tower in Paris in order to exculpate herself (vv. 36-38). Height, normally linked symbolically to superiority and spirituality, is here linked to humbling and to ignominy.

Hugo admits that the successful accomplishment of the three jests is indicative of God's love for Charles (v. 796), something which supporters of monarchy *gratia Dei* would have welcomed. With a nice comic touch, the poet has Charlemagne ask Hugo whether he wants any further *gabs* to be performed, to which he receives the reply 'Not this week' (vv. 799-800). The upshot of Hugo's submission is the procession in which the two kings wear their crowns together, a scene which was prepared as early as v. 20, in Charles's response to his wife's insult. Now, in condescending fashion, Charles agrees to wear his crown as a mark of friendship for King Hugo (v. 806). Not for the first time he is less than entirely honest. But now that the period of anxiety has passed, there is a marked change in the atmosphere. Once more there is enjoyment and celebration (v. 804). The crown-wearing ceremony itself, like other elements in the poem, has a dimension which can be measured precisely: compared to Charles, Hugo wears his crown 'plus basement un poi' (v. 810) and Charles is taller than Hugo by one foot three inches (v. 811). The concept of power is now conveyed mathematically and the point is of sufficient importance for it to be repeated: Hugo wears his crown lower than Charles (v. 817). The adverb *plus* conveys the concepts of comparison and superiority and it was first introduced in such a function by Charles's wife (vv. 14, 16, 27). We must also not forget that there is a third crown-wearer in the poem,

God, and he is also present at this ceremony by implication. One of the relics given to Charles in Jerusalem (and one of the two he will select for the altar at Saint-Denis, v. 866) is the crown worn by Christ (v. 176), and behind the present crowning ceremony lies God's love for the Franks ('Jo sai ke Deus vus aime', v. 796).[16] Just as the crowns of the two kings are signs of temporal power and authority, the third crown is a sign of Christ's kingdom which, in Biblical terms, is not like the kingdoms of this world (John 18: 36). Whatever the precise nature of its comic elements, this poem gives us constant reminders of its spiritual dimension.

It is difficult to know whether in these scenes the measurement of power in inches should be interpreted as a comic or a serious element in the text. There are many aspects of human society in which the concept of height takes on symbolic significance (high society, high table, high flier, etc.). If one follows the argument of Alfred Adler, who relates the events of the *Pèlerinage* to the 'spirit of St-Denis' and to events and personages from the middle of the twelfth century, the numerical precision of Charles's success is of particular significance 'Historically, the issue of whether Louis VII or Manuel of Constantinople was ranked higher or lower was a pointed one. Not only was Louis required or allowed his barons to be required to do homage and swear fealty to Manuel in Constantinople, but according to the Greek historian Kinnamos, Louis actually occupied a seat lower than Manuel's' (pp. 551-52).

The two references to Charlemagne's mathematically expressed superiority over Hugo (vv. 810, 817) are separated by a reminder of the opening scene. The Franks recall the queen's *folie* (v. 813), and Charles's initial confidence that he was superior to the foreign king (vv. 9-11) has now been vindicated by events (even if only by the grace of God). For the Franks, Charles's display of strength is prophetic. Wherever they go, they will always win the day (vv. 814-15). It is also to be noted that the Franks have done precisely what Charles envisaged them doing in vv. 20-23. They have witnessed two kings wearing their crowns together and articulated his superiority over his rival (v. 23). The plot has come full circle.

---

[16] In this poem God and Christ are subsumed within one entity, the term *Deus* being used to designate Christ in vv. 157, 176, etc.

Introduction

Like Charles's numerically precise superiority, the queen's folly is also mentioned for a second time. At this moment Charles's barons are basking in reflected glory: the queen was foolish, they say, when she scorned such fine barons as us (v. 820). The atmosphere is now and will remain one of great joy (vv. 830, 851, 858). For the Franks, normal service is resumed and again they enjoy food and wine in abundance. As happened on earlier occasions, nothing they require is slow in coming (v. 835, cf. vv. 247, 703). In similar fashion to the patriarch (vv. 222-23), Hugo offers the Franks all the treasure they can transport (vv. 839-40). It is now time for the Franks to depart. The ceremony of leave-taking operates in a similar way to that seen in the Jerusalem episode. Permission to leave is sought and given (v. 845, cf. vv. 216, 251) and the two kings embrace each other and entrust one another to God (vv. 847-48, cf. vv. 252-53). The one casualty of this happy ending is King Hugo's daughter. Too frightened of her father to speak to Oliver at the time of the procession (vv. 824-26), she is unable to restrain herself at the moment of departure. She rushes forward and grabs hold of Oliver. But to her re-affirmation of her love and her plea to him to take her back with him to France, he retorts that, although he loves her totally (v. 856), he must return without her (vv. 852-57). Perhaps somewhat strangely, it is on this note that the poet brings the Constantinople episode to an end. But by restoring the Oliver of the *Roland*, whose preoccupations are entirely feudal, the poet may be indicating that the narrative ends on a note of normality. In future the Franks will behave in more appropriate fashion and love will have no place in their lives.

(iv) Conclusion (vv. 858-70)

The text concludes with great brevity, only one laisse being required to bring it to an end. Charles is delighted by the outcome of his visit (v. 858) and the uneventful journey home is swiftly related (vv. 861-63). Charles places two of his relics, the nail and the crown, on the altar of Saint-Denis (v. 866). His choice of relics confirms that Christ, the third crown-wearer of this text, will be even more of a presence at Saint-Denis. Has Charles the Great now realized that true greatness lies in Heaven? Manifesting his willingness to share his success with others, he later distributes the rest of the relics throughout the kingdom. The queen, who no doubt fears the worst, falls at his feet (v. 868, cf. v. 31).

This is followed by the statement that 'Sun mautalent li ad li reis tut perdunét' (v. 869), which almost certainly means 'The king has abandoned his anger against her' rather than, as some translators would have it, 'The king has completely forgiven her spite'. This looks more like a reprieve than a full pardon. The last statement of the poem provides the reason for Charles's action in respect of the queen: he has adored the Holy Sepulchre (v. 870). Surprisingly, there is no specific mention of this within the narrative and perhaps yet again Charles is being economical with the truth. Even if he had learned some important truths on his travels, one can only wonder what account of his adventures in Constantinople he gave to those left at home!

General Conclusions

Are we dealing with a purely comic text or with one which has moral, didactic or political intent? Is the *Pèlerinage* a fundamentally humorous poem with some serious elements or a fundamentally serious text with some humorous elements? Perhaps it is a more or less balanced combination of the two, for a mingling of the *seria* with the *ludicra* was certainly not forbidden to a medieval writer. If, as Charlemagne has it, the *gabs* contain an strong element of playfulness (v. 655), there may be a similar element in the poem as it is presented to us.

On the face of it, the subject-matter of the text is more serious than comic. Quarrels between an emperor and his queen, threats of decapitation, visits to foreign countries and miracles performed through the power of Christian relics are not inherently comic. The overall theme of the poem might be deemed to be the struggle for power in the feudal world, a world in which all acts have spiritual implications. When King Hugo decides that he has suffered enough, he offers to become Charlemagne's vassal and to hold his kingdom from him as a fief (v. 787), an offer which he repeats on descending from his tower (v. 797). This is the sort of capitulation which epic heroes normally receive after a long struggle and it is reminiscent of Marsile's offer to Charlemagne in the *Chanson de Roland* (vv. 223-24). In our text the offer comes as a result of God's grace and after a chastening lesson. Horrent is perhaps therefore correct when he writes of the poem's 'grave sujet politique' (p. 113).

But the idea that Charlemagne, or any emperor, could be knocked off his feet by a revolving floor, or forced to flee to the top of a pine tree, does not suggest at first sight that the story is being presented in an inherently serious fashion. What of the sexual boasts of the wise and courtly Oliver? Such elements, however, did not prevent Coulet from taking the view that the *Pèlerinage* is a moral poem, and this view can be seen as supported by the intervention of the poet when he comments that Charles was right to spare Hugo any further humiliation (v. 789). The Franks are certainly humbled on more than one occasion and the poet criticises the mercantile activity connected with the church of La Latanie (vv. 210-13). More importantly, the angel brings the Franks a message from God that they should avoid foolish behaviour and never again jest at others' expense (vv. 675-76). The author is clearly aware of the danger of hubris and of the risks entailed if one forgets Christian humility, and the poem undoubtedly provides a number of lessons in the art of sensible behaviour. When he comments that Charles kept his promise to the patriarch and went to Spain to mount an offensive against the Saracens (v. 231), the author is reminding his audience of the importance of words, faith and commitment in the feudal world. God's commitment to the Frankish cause and Charles's commitment to God fashion a satisfying whole.

The challenge to the reader of this text is to cope not only with what the text says but also with how it has been interpreted. A number of approaches are conveniently summarized for us by Süpek: 'Le poème a été, tour à tour, considéré comme héroï-comique, rieur, sérieux, parisien d'esprit, anglais de coeur, oeuvre monacale, anticlérical, guerrier, antimilitariste, laudatif, défavorable, reflet doré de Byzance, pamphlet politique, parodie littéraire, satire historique' (p. 4). Many critics see the work as a parody: e.g. 'The work seems to parody, to mock the heroic virtues and exploits of Charlemagne' (Burrell, p. 53); 'The parodic intent of the poem is unquestionable' (Cobby, *Ambivalent Conventions*, p. 158). Others prefer to speak of humour: e.g. 'This humor ... seems free of any parodic or caricatural intent, because in the work there is no deliberate attempt at distortion or mockery' (Picherit, edition, p. iv). Yet others stress the serious issues which the poem raises. Bennett sees in the way in which Charles's victory is presented a prescription for the future of chivalry itself. The knight's virtues must be those of the *miles Christi*, who puts his prowess at the service of God, and they must be coupled with those of the *miles curialis*, the knight who is fully conversant with the needs of the court ('*Le Pèlerinage de Charlemagne*: le sens de l'aventure', p. 487). In Bennett's view, the poet puts forward these serious points in the form of a light-hearted and seductive tale rather than in that of an off-putting sermon. This is certainly a very tempting point of view. The overall message of the poem, conveyed in a truly comic spirit, could be that true Christian kingship and *militia*, so easily damaged by folly and hubris, are characterized by the maintenance of feudal values, the practice of humility and an awareness of dependency on divine support.

Genre

Superficially at least, the *Pèlerinage de Charlemagne* is a *chanson de geste*. Like many such *chansons*, it is composed in laisses, sections of unequal length sharing the same assonance. In the present edition, there are fifty-five laisses with an average length of just under sixteen lines (some editors do not separate vv. 226-32 into two laisses and consequently have fifty-four laisses). The traditional ten-syllable line of the *chanson de geste* has here become a twelve-syllable line, with a considerable number of exceptions (see Horrent, *Le Pèlerinage de Charlemagne*, pp. 127-28).

The principal characters in this poem, Charlemagne and his peers, are those of the *chanson de geste*. Unusually, they belong to two different epic cycles, the *geste du roi* and the *geste de Guillaume d'Orange* (or *de Garin de Monglane*). Charlemagne, Roland, Oliver and Gerin would have been known to a contemporary audience from the *Chanson de Roland*. Turpin and Naimes also appear in the *Roland*, but there they are not part of the group of twelve peers. Moreover, there is a clear reference to the Roland tradition when the patriarch of Jerusalem alludes to the threat posed by Saracens and pagans, who are out to destroy Christianity (vv. 224-25). In v. 232 we are reminded of the death of Roland and his twelve peers (a curious element for the author to introduce into his story if his primary aim was to parody the epic tradition).

Charles and the Franks make untypical epic heroes. Presented as pilgrims, they fall foul of King Hugo through their own folly and narrowly escape decapitation. The contrast with a tradition in which the peers die heroically for the sake of Christianity is considerable. But the association with this tradition provides the perspective by which we can judge events. The poet certainly saw his work as part of a wider whole and clearly envisaged

Charlemagne's activities in the *Pèlerinage* as a stage on the road to a Christian victory over paganism. What happens in this poem constitutes a happy prelude to the tragic loss of life which the defeat of the Saracens will entail.

A theme which is on permanent display in the *chansons de geste*, but absent in this poem, is warfare. The poet does refer to Charles's delight at having defeated Hugo without pitched battle (v. 859), but the Franks' lack of weapons is a significant feature in the way the poem is constructed. Although keen to make further conquests (v. 11), Charles did not leave France with the intention of putting his rival to the test on the battlefield. Should we therefore conclude that these pilgrims, armed with staffs and scrips, are not in fact heroes of a *chanson de geste*? Are we to look elsewhere for a genre to which to assign this work?

Should we classify the poem as a romance? Webster argues that the visit to Constantinople contains echoes of an Otherworld journey to a fairy realm, one in which the visitors are obliged to undergo prodigious tests, and Cross sees parallels between some of the *gabs* and the feats performed by Irish heroes such as Cuchulainn. Such factors, whatever their individual validity, suggest the world of Arthurian literature and courtly romance rather than the epic.[17] Certainly, King Hugo's beautiful and courtly daughter, with her blond hair and skin as white as a flower in summer, would make an excellent courtly heroine, and clad in shimmering silks and clinging to their lovers the three thousand comely maidens whom the Franks encounter on their arrival in Constantinople would grace any romance (vv. 272-74). Moreover, Charles's motivation for his trip to Constantinople makes it more reminiscent of a romance quest than of a military campaign in the style of a *chanson de geste*.[18]

On the basis of its humorous elements, Gautier calls the *Pèlerinage* a 'fabliau épique' (II, p. 260). But the poem contains too many feudal and political themes for it to be classed as a fabliau. Gaston Paris calls it merely a 'curieuse composition' (pp. 3, 7) and Bédier

---

[17] Rejhon has linked King Hugo to the Welsh figure of Hu Gadarn ('Hu Gadarn: Folklore and Fabrication'). She also contends that the *Pèlerinage* in its present form stems from 'a Celtic story involving a love triangle, in its Welsh Arthurian form' and that this story was profoundly modified and fused with extant legends concerning Charlemagne, France's own hero ('The French Reception of a Celtic Motif', p. 361).

[18] The distinction between a *chanson de geste* and a romance is not always easy to make. See for example the chapter 'Epic or Romance? Some Theoretical Implications' in Ellen R. Woods, *Aye d'Avignon: A Study of Genre and Society* (Geneva, 1978), pp. 59-71.

describes it in three ways, as an 'étrange petit roman', as 'la plus obscure des chansons de geste' and as a *gab* (IV, p. 151). For Bédier the poet's *gab* was 'une gageure de mêler le profane et le sacré, l'héroïque et le bouffon' (*ibid.*). More recently, Grigsby has argued that 'the *gabs* pervade the poem, its spirit, its structures' and that Charles's initial question to the queen is a *gab*. He therefore considers that the entire work should be classified as a *gab* ('A Note on the Genre', p. 8). But whichever of its elements we choose to stress, this poem remains difficult to define and classify. It seems preferable to avoid assigning it to any particular genre and to rejoice in its capacity to unite so many disparate features.

Sources and Influence

It is clearly not possible to determine precisely what texts and traditions influenced or inspired the author of the *Pèlerinage de Charlemagne*. Did he have just one major source for his tale or are we dealing with a combination of influences? It is likely that he was familiar with the *Descriptio*, the aim of which was to provide a description of and the source of the relics of the Passion held at Saint-Denis.[19] It tells how Charlemagne went to the East, at the request of the Greek emperor Constantine and the patriarch of Jerusalem, who were being besieged by the Saracens in Constantinople. Charles made his way to Constantinople, where he put the pagans to flight, then he liberated Jerusalem and subsequently returned to Constantinople. Although in recognition of his success he was offered a variety of gifts by King Constantine, Charlemagne preferred to depart from Constantinople with a number of relics of the Passion. These relics performed miracles before and during the journey back to Aix-la-Chapelle, and once there Charles established a Lendit, an annual feast, so that they could be venerated. The feast took place during the summer ember-days in the second week of June. Later, Charles the Bald transferred some of these relics from Aix-la-Chapelle to other locations. The holy shroud was transferred to

---

[19]   The full title is *Descriptio qualiter Karolus Magnus clavum et coronam Domini a Constantinopoli Aquisgrani detulerit qualiterque Karolus Calvus hec ad Sanctum Dyonisium retulerit* ('Description of how Charlemagne took the Nail and the Lord's Crown from Constantinople to Aix-la-Chapelle and how Charles the Bald transferred these to Saint-Denis'). For the text, see Ferdinand Castets, '*Iter Hierosolymitanum* ou *Voyage de Charlemagne à Jérusalem et à Constantinople*', *Revue des Langues Romanes*, 36 (1892), 439-74. See also R. Folz, *Le Souvenir et la légende de Charlemagne dans l'empire germanique médiéval* (Paris: Les Belles Lettres, 1950).

Saint-Cornelius of Compiègne and a nail from the Cross, the crown of thorns and a fragment of the cross went to Saint-Denis, to which the Lendit was also transferred. The Saint-Denis relics were also venerated during the summer ember-days, in conjunction with the Lendit.

The account of the transfer of relics in the *Descriptio* differs greatly from the detail of the plot of the *Pèlerinage*. Bédier, who made a very careful study of the *Descriptio* (IV, pp. 122-56), concluded that the author of the *Pèlerinage* may not even have read it. But one of the aims of the *Pèlerinage* could have been, like that of the *Descriptio*, to explain the origin of, and enhance the importance of, certain relics housed at the Abbey of Saint-Denis. Walpole thought that the author of the *Pèlerinage* was directly inspired by the *Descriptio* in the sense that it was a 'violent and independent reaction' to it (*'Le Pèlerinage de Charlemagne*: Jules Horrent and its "réalité cachée"', p. 182), and for him the *Pèlerinage* is 'a parody not of the French epic legend but of the *Descriptio*' (p. 183). If the author of the *Pèlerinage* was influenced by the *Descriptio*, the our poem must date from after 1110, the earliest possible date for the composition of the *Descriptio* (Bédier, IV, p. 139).

Charlemagne's adventures in Jerusalem and Constantinople, found in both the *Descriptio* and the *Pèlerinage*, are certainly not based on reality, for Charlemagne himself never travelled to either of these cities. But the authors may have been influenced by a legend which said that he did. Around the year 968 an Italian monk by the name of Benedictus of St Andrea wrote a chronicle in which he states that Charlemagne journeyed to the East in order to bring back relics. Charlemagne is said to have travelled to Jerusalem and on his way back to have visited Constantinople, where he concluded an alliance with the emperors Nicephorus, Michael and Leo. He then made his way to Italy where he was crowned emperor by the Pope. The relic of the body of St Andrea, which Charles had received from the Emperors of Constantinople, was presented to the monks of Mount Soracte.[20] This chronicle seems to be based on chapter XVI of Einhard's *Vita Caroli Magni*. Einhard had stated that Charlemagne established relations with the King of the Persians (Harun al-Rashid) through various embassies. The legend of a visit by Charles to the East reappears at the time of the First Crusade, when some crusaders thought that they

---

[20] See Aebischer, *Versions norroises*, pp. 110-11, and Giuseppe Zucchetti, *Il Chronicon di Benedetto Monaco di S. Andrea del Soratte e il Libellus de Imperatoria Potestate in Urbe Roma* (Rome, 1920), pp. 113-16.

were following in the emperor's footsteps. Charlemagne certainly seems to have been on excellent terms with eastern potentates. He received gifts and relics from Jerusalem, including the keys to the Holy Sepulchre and Calvary, and in 801 and 807 Harun al-Raschid sent ambassadors to him with splendid gifts.[21]

The difficulty in dating the *Pèlerinage* renders it more or less impossible to know precisely which literary works and traditions the poet could have known and used. It is certain that he knew the Roland tradition and that he had some knowledge of stories relating to the cycle of Guillaume d'Orange. As we have seen, several scholars have linked the poem to Celtic material and traditions and, if indeed it dates from well into the second half of the twelfth century, it is reasonable to expect that the author would have known and exploited links with the courtly romance. Popular tradition and oral accounts from visitors to Jerusalem and Constantinople might also have come the way of the author and helped him to fashion his text.

There are later French versions of the story of Charles's pilgrimage: *Galien le Restoré*, Girart d'Amiens' *Charlemagne* and the cyclical *Garin de Monglane*. There is also an abbreviated Old Norse translation in Branch I of the *Karlamagnús saga*. This compilation in Old Norse dates from the thirteenth century and Branch VII includes a version of particular interest, as it is close to that of the *Pèlerinage* itself. There is even a third version in Branch X, which is based on Vincent of Beauvais' *Speculum Historiale*. Although in the forms in which we have them they are later than the *Pèlerinage*, some of these versions could have had sources which pre-date our text. It could even be that there existed an earlier, entirely serious version of the story, which was preserved in Scandinavia and Spain, and that the *Pèlerinage* as we have it resulted from the fusion of this serious tradition with other sources, notably with a Celtic tale relating the abduction of Guinevere and the rivalry between King Arthur and an Otherworld king.[22]

---

[21] See Charles Runciman, 'Charlemagne and Palestine', *English Historical Review*, 50 (1935), 606-19, and Lewis Thorpe, *Einhard and Notker the Stammerer: Two Lives of Charlemagne* (Harmondsworth: Penguin Books, 1969), pp. 70-71.

[22] See Rejhon, 'The French Reception of a Celtic Motif', p. 352, and Jules Horrent, *Roncesvalles: étude sur le fragment de cantar de gesta conservé à l'Archivo de Navarra (Pampelune)* (Paris: Les Belles Lettres, 1951), pp. 196-203 (here Charles is said to have journeyed to Jerusalem in the company of Roland).

The Present Text and Translation

There can be few texts which have regularly appeared in modern editions in such a highly emended form. Our text, however, is minimally edited and we have intervened only in cases of obvious scribal error.[23] No attempt has been made to correct either syllable-count or faulty assonance and we have been reluctant to correct either the grammar or the morphology of the text. The many dialectal and variant spellings have deliberately been preserved. In general, the text has been corrected only when failure to do so would interfere with the understanding of the passage concerned. Rejected readings are given at the foot of the page. Abbreviations have been expanded in accordance with normal editorial practice: *i* and *j* have been kept separate, as have *u* and *v*. Where necessary, to distinguish a soft *c* from a hard *c*, a cedilla has been employed, and an acute accent has been used when required to distinguish tonic from atonic *e*. When *e* is elided before a vowel, this is signalled by the use of an apostrophe. It has been necessary to provide punctuation, to capitalise and on occasion to divide words in accordance with normal principles. Proper names have been expanded when they were abbreviated in the original MS.

The line-by-line translation aims to offer a straightforward version of the text in modern English. Each line of text is rendered by one line of translation. Where necessary, elements within a line have been rearranged to give the English a more satisfactory rhythm. In spite of the fact that shifts of tense can be slightly disconcerting in English, the tenses of the original have been maintained, in order to preserve the time sequences as they are presented in the original.[24]

---

[23] Michel's edition of 1836, the only one to be based directly on the manuscript, is likewise very conservative. If we take, for example, the first three lines of the text, Michel made no changes, whereas Koschwitz in his first edition of 1880 made thirteen minor changes plus the transformation of the form *Karleun* into *Carlemaigne*. In his second edition of 1883 Koschwitz made seventeen changes, including the change from *li puinz (en)* to *dont li ponz* in v. 3, plus a new emendation of *Karleun* in v. 1 to *li reis Charles*.

[24] For details concerning the language and versification of the text, readers should consult, in particular, Favati's edition, Horrent (*Le Pèlerinage de Charlemagne: essai d'explication littéraire*, pp. 127-50), Koschwitz (*Überlieferung und Sprache* and the introductions to his editions) and Tyssens (pp. 30-84).

SELECT BIBLIOGRAPHY

EDITIONS AND TRANSLATIONS

Aebischer, Paul, *Le Voyage de Charlemagne à Jérusalem et à Constantinople.* Textes Littéraires Français, 115 (Geneva: Droz; Paris: Minard, 1965, 2nd edn, 1971).

Bonafin, Massimo, *Il Viaggio di Carlomagno in Oriente*, Bibliotheca Medievale, 3 (Parma: Pratiche, 1987). Includes a facing translation in Italian.

Burgess, Glyn S., and Anne Elizabeth Cobby, *The Pilgrimage of Charlemagne (Le Pèlerinage de Charlemagne): Aucassin and Nicolette (Aucassin et Nicolette)*, Garland Library of Medieval Literature, series A, 47 (New York and London: Garland Publishing, 1988). Includes a facing prose translation in English by G. S. Burgess (pp. 29-71) and an Introduction by A. E. Cobby (pp. 1-16).

Cavalieri, Alfredo, *Il Pellegrinaggio di Carlomagno a Gerusalemme e a Costantinopli* (Venice: Libraria Universitaria, 1965). Includes a facing translation in Italian.

Cooper, Anna J., *Le Pèlerinage de Charlemagne* (Paris: Lahure, 1925). Includes a translation in Modern French.

Favati, Guido, *Il Voyage de Charlemagne: edizione critica*, Biblioteca degli Studi Mediolatini e Volgari, 4 (Bologna: Palmaverde, 1965). Includes a translation in Italian.

Koschwitz, Eduard, *Karls des Grossen Reise nach Jerusalem und Constantinopel: ein altfranzösisches Gedicht des XI. Jahrhunderts*, Altfranzösische Bibliothek, 2 (Heilbronn: Henninger, 1880).

---, *Karls des Grossen Reise nach Jerusalem und Constantinopel: ein altfranzösisches Heldengedicht*, Altfranzösische Bibliothek, 2 (2nd edn Heilbronn: Henninger, 1883, 3rd edn, 1895, 4th edn, 1900. 5th edn, revised by Gustav Thurau, Leipzig: Reisland, 1907, 6th edn, 1913, 7th edn, 1923. The second and subsequent editions are less conservative than the first. They contain a diplomatic edition of the text and a facing, highly emended edition. The 6th and 7th editions are a reprint of the 5th edition.

Michel, Francisque, *Charlemagne: An Anglo-Norman Poem of the Twelfth Century* (London: Pickering; Paris: Techener, 1836). The earliest edition of the text, accompanied by a lengthy Preface (pp. i-cxv) and a glossarial index (pp. 39-145).

Picherit, Jean-Louis, G., *The Journey of Charlemagne to Jerusalem and Constantinople (Le Voyage de Charlemagne à Jérusalem et à Constantinople)* (Birmingham, Alabama: Summa Publications, 1984). Includes a facing line-by-line translation in English.

Bibliography

Riquer, Isabel de, *Le Pèlerinage de Charlemagne / La Peregrinación de Carlomagno*, Biblioteca Filológica, 3 (Barcelona: El Festín de Esopo, 1984). Includes a facing translation in Spanish prose.

Schlauch, Margaret, *Medieval Narrative: A Book of Translations* (New York: Prentice-Hall, 1928, repr. New York: Gordian Press, 1969). Includes a prose translation in English (pp. 77-101).

Tyssens, Madeleine, *Le Voyage de Charlemagne à Jérusalem et à Constantinople: traduction critique*, Ktemata, 3 (Ghent: Story-Scientia, 1978). A line-by-line translation in Modern French with extensive critical notes. No text included.

OTHER VERSIONS

Aebischer, Paul, *Textes norrois et littérature française du moyen âge, I* (Geneva and Lille: Droz, 1954).

Hieatt, Constance B., *Karlamagnús saga: the Saga of Charlemagne and his Heroes*, 3 vols (Toronto: Pontifical Institute of Mediaeval Studies, 1975-80).

Koschwitz, Eduard, *Sechs Bearbeitungen des altfranzösischen Gedichts von Karls des Grossen Reise nach Jerusalem und Constantinopel* (Heilbronn: Henninger, 1879).

Togeby, Knud, Pierre Helleux, Agnete Loth and Annette Patron-Godefroit, *Karlamagnús Saga, Branches I, III, VII et IX* (Copenhagen: Reitzels, 1980).

Williams, Stephen J., *Ystorya de Carolo Magno o Lyfr Coch Hergest* (Cardiff: Gwasg Prifysgol Cymru, 1962, rev. ed. 1968).

ARTICLES AND BOOKS

Adler, Alfred, 'The *Pèlerinage de Charlemagne* in New Light on Saint-Denis', *Speculum*, 22 (1947), 550-61.

Aebischer, Paul, 'Le *gab* d'Olivier', *Revue Belge de Philologie et d'Histoire*, 34 (1956), 659-79.

---, *Les Versions norroises du Voyage de Charlemagne en Orient: leurs sources* (Paris: Les Belles Lettres, 1956).

---, 'Sur Quelques Passages du *Voyage de Charlemagne à Jérusalem et à Constantinople*: à propos d'un livre récent', *Revue Belge de Philologie et d'Histoire*, 40 (1962), 815-43.

Bates, Robert C., '*Le Pèlerinage de Charlemagne*: A Baroque Epic', *Yale Romanic Studies*, 18 (1941), 1-47.

Beckmann, Gustav A., 'Hugue li Forz: zur Genesis einer literarischen Gestalt', *Zeitschrift für französische Sprache und Literatur*, 81 (1971), 289-307.

Bennett, Philip E., '*Le Pèlerinage de Charlemagne*: le sens de l'aventure', in *Essor et fortune de la chanson de geste dans l'Europe et l'Orient latin: actes du IXe congrès international de la Société Rencesvals pour l'étude des épopées romanes, Padoue-Venise, 29 août-4 septembre 1982* (Modena: Mucchi, 1984), pp. 475-87.

---, '*La grant ewe del flum*: Toponomy and Text in *Le Pèlerinage de Charlemagne*', in *The Editor and the Text*, ed. by P. E. Bennett and G. A. Runnalls (Edinburgh: Edinburgh University Press, 1990), pp. 125-36.

---, '"Si vus en respondrai volenters par guionage" (*Le Voyage de Charlemagne*, v. 658)', *Romania*, 112 (1991), 540-43.

Bonafin, Massimo, 'Fiaba e *chanson de geste*: note in margine a une lettura del *Voyage de Charlemagne*', *Medioevo Romanzo*, 9 (1984), 3-16.

---, *La Tradizione del Voyage de Charlemagne e il gabbo* (Allessandria: Orso, 1990).

Brians, Paul, 'Paul Aebischer and the "Gab d'Olivier"', *Romance Notes*, 15 (1973-74), 164-71.

Burgess, Glyn S., 'Old French *contenance* and *contenant*', in *Voices of Conscience: Essays in Memory of James D. Powell and Rosemary Hodgkins* (Philadelphia: Temple University Press, 1977), pp. 21-41.

---, '"Ne n'out Crisans de Rome, qui tanz honurs bastid" (*Pèlerinage de Charlemagne*, v. 367)', in *Actes du XIe congrès international de la Société Rencesvals (Barcelone, 22-27 août 1988)*, 2 vols (Barcelona: Real Academia de Buenas Letras, 1990), I, pp. 103-20.

---, 'The Term *courtois* in Twelfth-Century French', in *Etudes de lexicologie, lexicographie et stylistique offertes en hommage à Georges Matoré* (Paris: L'Information Grammaticale, 1987), pp. 105-22. Also published in French as 'Le terme *cortois* dans le français du douzième siècle', *Travaux de Linguistique et de Philologie*, 31 (1993), 195-209.

Burns, E. Jane, 'Portraits of Kingship in the *Pèlerinage de Charlemagne*', *Olifant*, 10 (1982-85), 161-81.

Burrell, Margaret, 'The *Voyage of Charlemagne*: Cultural Transmission or Cultural Transgression?', *Parergon*, new series, 7 (1989), 47-53.

---, 'The Specular Heroine: Self-Creation versus Silence in *Le Pèlerinage de Charlemagne* and *Erec et Enide*', *Parergon*, 15 (1997), 85-99.

Bibliography

Carmody, Francis J., *Le Pèlerinage de Charlemagne: sources et parallèles* (Greenbrae, California: The Author, 1976).

Caulkins, Janet H., 'Narrative Interventions: the Key to the *Jest* of the *Pèlerinage de Charlemagne*', in *Etudes de philologie romane et d'histoire littéraire offertes à Jules Horrent à l'occasion de son soixantième anniversaire* (Liège, 1980), pp. 47-55.

Ceron, Sandra, 'Un *gap* épique: *Le Pèlerinage de Charlemagne*', *Medioevo Romanzo*, 11 (1986), 175-91.

Cobby, Anne Elizabeth, 'Religious Elements in *Le Voyage de Charlemagne à Jérusalem et à Constantinople*', in *Au Carrefour des routes d'Europe: la chanson de geste, Xᵉ congrès international de la Société Rencesvals pour l'étude des épopées romanes (Strasbourg, 1985)*, 2 vols (Aix-en-Provence: Université de Provence, 1987), I, 367-82.

---, *Ambivalent Conventions: Formula and Parody in Old French* (Amsterdam: Rodopi, 1995).

Coulet, Jules, *Etudes sur l'ancien poème français du Voyage de Charlemagne en Orient* (Montpellier: Coulet et Fils, 1907).

Cromie, Maureen, 'Le Style formulaire dans *Le Voyage de Charlemagne à Jérusalem et à Constantinople (Le Pèlerinage de Charlemagne)*', *Revue des Langues Romanes*, 77 (1967), 31-54.

Cross, Tom Peete, 'The Gabs', *Modern Philology*, 25 (1927-28), 349-54.

De La Rue, Abbé Gervais, *Essais historiques sur les bardes, les jongleurs et les trouvères normands et anglo-normands*, 3 vols (Caen: Mancel, 1834), II, 23-32.

Denusianu, O., 'Aymeri de Narbonne dans la chanson du *Pèlerinage de Charlemagne*', *Romania*, 25 (1896), 481-96.

Deroy, Jean, 'Respect du code de l'amour dans le gab d'Olivier', in *Société Rencesvals pour l'étude des épopées romanes, VIᵉ congrès international (Aix-en-Provence, 29 août-4 septembre 1973): Actes* (Aix-en-Provence: Université de Provence, 1974), pp. 241-51.

Frings, Th., Review of P. Aebischer, *Textes norrois, I*, in *Zeitschrift für romanische Philologie*, 83 (1957), 175-83.

Gännsle-Pfeuffer, Cäcilie, '*Majestez* und *vertu* in der *Karlsreise*: zur Problematik der Deutung der Dichtung', *Zeitschrift für romanische Philologie*, 83 (1967), 257-67.

Bibliography

Gautier, Léon, *Les Epopées françaises: étude sur les origines et l'histoire de la littérature nationale*, 3 vols (Paris: Société Générale de Librairie Catholique, 1865-68), II, 260-305, 2nd edn, 4 vols, 1878-94, III, 270-315.

Gosman, Martin, 'La Propagande politique dans *Le Voyage de Charlemagne à Jérusalem et à Constantinople*', *Zeitschrift für romanische Philologie*, 102 (1986), 53-66.

Grigsby, John L., 'A Note on the Genre of the *Voyage de Charlemagne*', in *Essays in Early French Literature Presented to Barbara M. Craig* (York, South Carolina: French Literature Publications, 1982), pp. 1-8.

---, 'The Relics' Rôle in the *Voyage de Charlemagne*', *Olifant*, 9 (1981-82), 20-34.

---, '*Le Voyage de Charlemagne*, pèlerinage ou parodie?', in *Au Carrefour des routes d'Europe: la chanson de geste, X^e congrès international de la Société Rencesvals pour l'étude des épopées romanes (Strasbourg, 1985)*, 2 vols (Aix-en-Provence: Université de Provence, 1987), I, 567-84.

Hatcher, Anna Granville, 'Contributions to the *Pèlerinage de Charlemagne*', *Studies in Philology*, 44 (1947), 4-25.

Heinermann, Theodor, 'Zeit und Sinn der *Karlsreise*', *Zeitschrift für romanische Philologie*, 56 (1936), 497-562.

Holmes, Urban T., 'The *Pèlerinage de Charlemagne* and William of Malmsebury', *Symposium*, 1 (1946-47), 75-81.

Horrent, Jules, 'La Chanson du *Pèlerinage de Charlemagne*: problèmes de composition', in *La Technique littéraire des chansons de geste: actes du colloque de Liège (septembre 1957)* (Paris: Les Belles Lettres, 1959), pp. 409-28.

---, 'Sur les sources épiques du *Pèlerinage de Charlemagne*', *Revue Belge de Philologie et d'Histoire*, 38 (1960), 750-64.

---, *Le Pèlerinage de Charlemagne: essai d'explication littéraire avec des notes de critique textuelle* (Paris: Les Belles Lettres, 1961).

---, 'Contribution à l'établissement du texte perdu du *Pèlerinage de Charlemagne*', in *Studi in onore di Italo Siciliano*, 2 vols (Florence: Olschi, 1966), pp. 557-79.

Knudson, Charles A., 'A "Distinctive and Charming Jewel": *Le Voyage de Charlemagne à Jérusalem et à Constantinople*', *Romanic Review*, 59 (1968), 98-105.

Koschwitz, Eduard, 'Über das Alter und die Herkunft der *Chanson du Voyage de Charlemagne à Jérusalem et à Constantinople*', *Romanische Studien*, 2 (1875-77), 1-60.

Leupin, Alexandre, 'La Compromission (sur *Le Voyage de Charlemagne à Jérusalem et à Constantinople)*', *Romance Notes*, 25 (1984-85), 222-38.

Levy, Raphael, 'Sur le vers 384 du *Pèlerinage de Charlemagne*', *Romania*, 64 (1938), 102-04.

---, 'The Term "language" in *Le Pèlerinage de Charlemagne*', *Modern Language Notes*, 62 (1947), 125-27.

Loomis, Laura Hibbard, 'Observations on the *Pèlerinage Charlemagne*', *Modern Philology*, 25 (1927-28), 331-49.

Méla, Charles, 'Immobile, à grands pas: Charlemagne en Orient', *Revue des Sciences Humaines*, 214 (1989), 9-24.

Morf, H., 'Etude sur la date, le caractère et l'origine de la chanson du *Pèlerinage de Charlemagne*', *Romania*, 13 (1884), 185-232.

Neuschäfer, Hans-Jörg, '*Le Voyage de Charlemagne en Orient* als Parodie der *chanson de geste*: Untersuchungen zur Epenparodie im Mittelalter (I)', *Romanistisches Jahrbuch*, 10 (1959), 78-102.

Nicholls, J. A., 'The *Voyage de Charlemagne*: A Suggested Reading of Lines 100-108', *Australian Journal of French Studies*, 16 (1979), 270-77.

Nicol, Henry, Review of Koschwitz, 1st edn, *The Academy*, 19 (1881), 139-40.

Niles, John D., 'On the Logic of *Le Pèlerinage de Charlemagne*', *Neuphilologische Mitteilungen*, 81 (1980), 208-16.

Owen, D. D. R., '*Voyage de Charlemagne* and *Chanson de Roland*', *Studi Francesi*, 11 (1967), 468-72.

Panvini, Bruno, 'Ancora sul *Pèlerinage de Charlemagne*', *Siculorum Gymnasium*, new series, 13 (1960), 17-80.

---, *Il Pèlerinage Charlemagne* (Catania: CUESCM, 1983).

Paris, Gaston, 'La Chanson du *Pèlerinage de Charlemagne*', *Romania*, 9 (1880), 1-50.

Pinson, M., 'Un nouvel Essai d'explication: *Pèlerinage de Charlemagne* vv. 100-08', *Romanische Forschungen*, 89 (1977), 266-68.

Pioletti, Antonio, 'Carlo-Ugo e la parodia nel *Voyage de Charlemagne*', *Messana*, 6 (1991), 5-29.

Polak, Lucie, 'Charlemagne and the Marvels of Constantinople', in *The Medieval Alexander Legend and Romance Epic: Essays in Honour of David J.A. Ross* (Millwood, New York: Kraus International, 1982), pp. 159-71.

Rejhon, Annalee C., 'Hu Gadarn: Folklore and Fabrication', in *Celtic Folklore and Christianity: Studies in Memory of William W. Heist* (Santa Barbara: McNally and Loftin, 1983), pp. 201-12.

---, 'The French Reception of a Celtic Motif: The *Pèlerinage de Charlemagne à Jérusalem et à Constantinople*', *Zeitschrift für celtische Philologie*, 42 (1987), 344-61.

Richard, Jean, 'Sur un Passage du *Pèlerinage de Charlemagne*: le marché de Jérusalem', *Revue Belge de Philologie et d'Histoire*, 43 (1965), 552-55.

Rossman, Vladimir R., *Perspectives of Irony in Medieval French Literature* (The Hague: Mouton, 1975).

Scheludko, D., 'Zur Komposition der *Karlsreise*', *Zeitschrift für romanische Philologie*, 53 (1933), 317-25.

Schlauch, Margaret, 'The Palace of Hugon de Constantinople', *Speculum*, 7 (1932), 500-14.

Spitzer, Leo, '*Lenguages* dans le *Pèlerinage de Charlemagne*, v. 209', *Modern Language Notes*, 53 (1938), 20-21, 553.

Sturm, Sara, 'The Stature of Charlemagne in the *Pèlerinage*', *Studies in Philology*, 71 (1974), 1-18.

Suchier, Hermann, 'La XIVe laisse du *Voyage de Charlemagne*', *Le Moyen Age*, 1 (1888), 10-11.

Süpek, Ottó, 'Une Parodie royale du moyen âge', *Annales Universitatis Scientiarum Budapestinensis de Rolando Eötvös Nominatae, Sectio Philologica Moderna*, 8 (1977), 3-25.

Torrini-Roblin, Gloria, '*Gomen* and *gab*: Two Models for Play in Medieval Literature', *Romance Philology*, 38 (1984-85), 32-40.

Trannoy, Patricia, 'De la technique à la magie: enjeu des automates dans *Le Voyage de Charlemagne à Jérusalem et à Constantinople*', in *Le Merveilleux et la magie dans la littérature: actes du colloque de Caen, 31 août-2 septembre 1989* (Amsterdam and Atlanta: Rodopi, 1992), pp. 227-52.

Van Belle, G., '*Le Voyage de Charlemagne à Jérusalem et à Constantinople*: pour une approche narratologique', *Revue Belge de Philologie et d'Histoire*, 64 (1986), 465-72.

Bibliography

Vance, Eugene, 'Semiotics and Power: Relics, Icons, and the *Voyage de Charlemagne à Jérusalem et à Constantinople*', *Romanic Review*, 79 (1988), 164-83. Reprinted in *The New Medievalism*, ed. by Marina S. Brownlee and others (Baltimore and London: The Johns Hopkins University Press, 1991), pp. 226-49.

Walpole, Ronald N., 'The *Pèlerinage de Charlemagne*: Poem, Legend, and Problem', *Romance Philology*, 8 (1954-55), 173-86.

---, '*Le Pèlerinage de Charlemagne*: Jules Horrent and its "réalité cachée"', *Romance Philology*, 17 (1963-64), 133-45.

Walton, Edward, 'The Palace of Hugon: Historical Allusion and Literary Reality in the *Pèlerinage de Charlemagne*', *Les Bonnes Feuilles*, 1 (1972), 26-33.

Le Pèlerinage de Charlemagne

The incipit and the opening lines of the *Pèlerinage de Charlemagne*
(taken from the edition published by F. Michel in 1836)

LE PELERINAGE DE CHARLEMAGNE

(THE PILGRIMAGE OF CHARLEMAGNE)

Ci comence le livere cumment Charels de Fraunce

voiet in Jerhusalem et pur parols sa feme a

Constantinnoble pur vere roy Hugon

(Here begins the book telling how Charles of France

travelled to Jerusalem and, because of the remarks

of his wife, to Constantinople to see King Hugo)

I

Un jur fu Karleun al Seint Denis muster;
Reout prise sa corune, en croiz seignat sun chef,
E ad ceinte sa espee, li ponz fud d'or mer.
Dux i out e demeines e baruns e chevalers.
5   Li empereres reguardet la reine sa muillers;
Ele fut ben corunee al plus bel e al meuz.
Il la prist par le poin desuz un oliver;
De la pleine parole la prist a reisuner:
'Dame, veistes unkes hume nul dedesuz ceil
10 Tant ben seist espee ne la corone el chef?
Uncore cunquerrai jo citez ot mun espeez.'
Cele ne fud pas sage, folement respondeit:
'Emperere', dist ele, 'trop vus poez preiser;
Uncore en sa jo un ki plus se fait leger,
15 Quant il porte corune entre ses chevalers.
Kaunt il la met sur sa teste, plus belement lui set.'
Quant l'entend Charle, mult est curecez;
Pur Franceis ki l'oirent mult est embrunchez.
'E, dame, u est cil reis? Kar le m'enseinez!
20 Si porterum ensemble les corunes as cheis,
Si i serrunt vos druz e tuz vos cunsilers.
Jo maunderai ma court de mes bons chevalers;
Si Franceis le me dient, dunc le otri jo ben.
Se vus me avez mentid, vus le cumperez cher.
25 Trencherai vus la teste od me espee d'acer.'
'Emperere', dist ele, 'ne vus en curucez!
Plus est riche de aver, d'or e de deners,
Mais n'est mie si pruz ne si bon chevalers
Pur ferir en bataile ne pur encaucer.'
30 Quant ce ot la reine ke Charles est si irrez,
Forment s'en repent, vuelt li chair as pez.

II

'Emperere', dist ele, 'mercid pur amur Deu.
Ja su ge vostre femme, si me quidai juer;
Jo m'escundirai ja, se vus le cumandez,
35 A jurer serement u juise a porter.
De la plus haulte tur de Paris la citez
Me larrai cuntreval par creance devaler

---

6 as m.   30 ce out   32 Empere   34 mescundirari

I

One day Charles was in the Church of Saint-Denis;
He had put on his crown and he crossed himself.
His sword was girt about him, its pommel was of pure gold.
There were dukes there, and lords, barons and knights.
5   The emperor looks at the queen, his wife:
She wore her crown in as fine a fashion as could be.
He took her by the hand beneath an olive tree;
In loud tones he began to address her:
'My lady, did you ever see any man on earth
10 Whose sword became him so, or the crown on his head?
I shall conquer yet more cities with my lance.'
The queen was not wise, she replied foolishly:
'Emperor', she said, 'you may regard yourself too highly.
I know someone who is even more dashing than you
15 When he wears his crown in the company of his knights.
When he puts it on his head, it suits him better.'
When Charles hears her, he is very angry;
Because of the Franks who had heard her, he bows his head low:
'Come, my lady, where is this king? Tell me who he is!
20 Then we shall wear our crowns together on our heads,
And your friends will be there and all your counsellors.
I shall summon my fine knights to court.
If the Franks say so, then I grant that it is so.
If you have lied to me, you will pay dearly for it;
25 I shall cut off your head with my sword of steel.'
'Emperor', she said, 'do not be angry at this!
He has greater wealth than you, in gold and in coin,
But he is not so valiant or such a fine knight
When it comes to striking on the battlefield or routing the enemy.'
30 When the queen hears that Charles is so angry,
She greatly regrets her words and is willing to fall at his feet.

II

'Emperor', she said, 'have pity for the love of God!
I am your wife and I meant this as a joke;
I shall clear myself of this at once, if you order me to,
35 By swearing an oath or submitting to an ordeal.
From the highest tower in the city of Paris
I shall allow myself to be thrown down,

Que pur la vostre hunte ne fud dit ne penséd.'
'Nu frez', dist Charle, 'mais le rei me numez!'
40   'Emperere', dist ele, 'ja nel puis jo truver.'
'Par mun chef', dist Carle, 'orendreit le me dirrez,
U jo vus frai ja cele teste couper.'

III

Ore entend la reine que ne se puet estortre;
Volenteres la leisast, mais que muer nen osed.
45   'Emperere', dist ele, 'ne me tenez a fole;
Del rei Hugun le Fort ai mult oi parole.
Emperere est de Grece e de Costuntinoble,
Il tent tute Perse tresque en Capadoce;
N'at tant bel chevaler de ci en Antioche.
50   Ne fut tel barnez cum le sun, senz le vostre.'
'Par mun chef', dist Carle, 'ço saverai jo uncore;
Se mençunge avez dite, a fiance estes morte.'

IV

'Par ma fei', dist li reis, 'mult m'aveiz irascud.
M'amistéd e mun gréd en avez tut perduz;
55   Uncore quid qu'en perderez la teste sur le buc.
Nel dusés ja penser, dame, de ma vertuz;
Ja n'en prenderai mais fin tresque l'averei veuz.'

V

Li emperere de France, cum il fud curunez
E out faite sa offrende a l'auter principel,
60   A la sale de Parys si s'en est retornez.
Rolland e Oliver en ad ot sei amenez
E Willeme de Orenge e Naimon l'adurez,
Oger de Denemarche, Berin e Berenger,
Le arceveske Turpin e Ernalz e Haimer,
65   E Bernard de Brusban e Bertram l'adurez,
E tel .m. chevaler ki sunt de France nez.
'Seignors', dist l'emperere, 'un petit m'entendez!
En un lointain reaume, si Deu pleist, en irrez
Jerusalem requere e la tere Damnedeu.
70   La croiz e le sepulcre voil aler aurer;
Jo l'ai trei feiz sungéd, moi i covent aler,

---

43 estorcer   56 ne duses; du ma   57 prenderari   65 bernand
69 la mere

To vouch to you that it was not said or thought to shame you.'
'No you will not', said Charles, 'just name me the king!'
40   'Emperor', she said, 'I cannot recall it.'
'By my head', said Charles, 'you will tell me it at once,
Or I shall have that head of yours cut off.'

III

Now the queen understands that she cannot evade the question.
She would gladly have let this drop, but she dares not change her story.
45   'Emperor', she said, 'do not think me a fool.
I have heard talk a great deal of King Hugo the Strong.
He is emperor of Greece and Constantinople.
He holds all Persia as far as Cappadocia,
There is no finer knight from here to Antioch.
50   There was never such a noble band of men as his, except for yours.'
'By my head', said Charles, 'I shall yet find out the truth of this;
If you have lied, you are a dead woman, I swear.'

IV

'Upon my word', said the king, 'you have angered me greatly.
You have completely lost my affection and my goodwill.
55   I still think that you will lose the head from your body.
You ought not, my lady, to have had such thoughts about my power.
I shall never rest until I have seen him.'

V

The Emperor of France, when he had worn his crown
And made his offering at the main altar,
60   Returned to the palace in Paris.
He took with him Roland and Oliver,
And William of Orange and the doughty Naimes,
Ogier of Denmark, Berin and Berenger,
Archbishop Turpin, Ernaut and Aimer,
65   Bernard of Brusban and the doughty Bertrand,
And some thousand knights who were born in France.
'My lords', said the emperor, 'listen to me for a moment;
You will go to a far-off kingdom, if it pleases God,
And visit Jerusalem and the land of the Lord God.
70   I wish to go and worship the cross and the sepulchre.
I have dreamed this three times, it is necessary for me to go.

E irrai un rei requerre dount ai oi parler.
Set .c. cameilz merrez, d'or e de argent trusséd,
Pur set aunz en la tere ester u demurer.
75   Ja ne m'en turnerai trescque l'averai trovez.'

VI

Li emperere de France feit cunreer sa gent
E ceols qui alerent od lui cunreat gentement.
Asez lur ad donez entre or fin e argent;
N'i unt escuz ne lances ne espees trenchaunz,
80   Mais fustz ferét de fraine e escrepes pendanz;
E funt ferrer les destrers detrés e devaunt.
Les mulz e les sumers afeutrent li servant
E funt pleines les males entre or fin e argent,
De veisaus e de deners e de autre garnement.
85   Faudestoulz d'or i portent e treis de seie blanc.
A Seint Denis de France li reis s'escrepe prent.
Li arcevesche Turpin li seignat gentement
E si prist il la sue e Franceis ensement,
E muntent as mulz qu'il orent forz e amblanz.
90   De la citez s'en isirent, si s'en turnent brochaunt;
Des ore s'en irrat Carles al Damnedeu cummant.
La reine remeint doloruse e pluraunt.
Tant chevauchet li reis qu'il vint en un plain;
A une part s'en turnet, si apelet Bertram:
95   'Veez cum gentes cumpaines de pelerins erraund!
E hitantes milies sunt el premer chef devant.
Ki ço duit e governet ben deit estre poant.'

VII

Ore vait li emperere od ses granz cumpainies;
Devant el premer chef furent oitante milz.
100   Il issirent de France e Burgoine guerpirent,
Loheregne traversent, Baivere e Hungerie,
Les Turcs e les Persaunz e cele gent haie.
La grant ewe del flum passerent a Lalice.
Chevauchet li emperere tres parmi Croiz Partie,
105   Les bois e les forez, e sunt entrez en Grece.
Les puis e les muntaines virent en Romanie
E brochent a la terre u Deus receut martirie;
Veient Jerusalem, une citez antive.

---

75 lauerari   78 entrere   81 destres de tres e devuant   91 i. cales a
damne Deu le c.   94 berteraram   103 a la liee

And I shall go and visit a king of whom I have heard talk.
You will take seven hundred camels, laden with gold and silver,
In order to stay and live for seven years in that land.
75   I shall not return until I have found him.'

VI

The Emperor of France has his companions equip themselves,
And those who went with him he equipped nobly.
He gave them large amounts of both pure gold and silver;
They have with them no shields, lances or sharp swords,
80   But staffs of ash tipped with iron and hanging scrips,
And they have their chargers shod front and rear.
The servants saddle the mules and the packhorses
And fill up the trunks with both pure gold and silver,
With vessels and coins and other equipment;
85   They carry golden thrones of state and tents of white silk.
At Saint-Denis of France the king takes up his scrip.
Archbishop Turpin blessed him in noble fashion
And he took up his own scrip, as did the Franks,
And they mount their sturdy, ambling mules.
90   They rode forth from the city and spurred away.
From now on Charles will travel under God's direction.
The queen remains behind, weeping sorrowfully.
The king rides on until he came to a plain;
He turns to one side and calls to Bertrand:
95   'See what a noble band of men these travelling pilgrims are!
There are eighty thousand men out in front;
The man who leads and governs them must indeed have great power.'

VII

Now the emperor journeys on with his great bands of men:
In the vanguard were eighty thousand men.
100 They left France and travelled through Burgundy,
They cross Lorraine, Bavaria and Hungary,
Through the Turks and the Persians and that accursed people;
They crossed the great river at Lycia.
On rides the emperor right through the area of the Cross,
105 Through woods and forests, and they entered Greece.
They saw the hills and the mountains of Romania
And they ride swiftly on to the land where Christ suffered martyrdom.
They catch sight of Jerusalem, an ancient city.

Li jours fu beaus e clers, herberges unt purprises,
110   E venent al muster, lur offerendes i unt mises;
As herberges repairent les feres cumpainies.

VIII

Mult est genz li presenz que Carles i offret.
Entrat en un muster de marbre peint a volte;
Laens ad un alter de saincte Paternostre.
115   Deus i chantat messe, si firent li apostle,
E les .xii. chaeres i sunt tutes uncore;
Li treezime est enmi, ben seelee e close.
Karle i entrat, ben out al queor grant joie.
Cum il vit la chaere, icele part s'aprocet:
120   L'emperere s'asist, un petit se reposet.
Li .xii. peers as altres, envirunt e en coste;
Ainz n'i sist hume, ne unkes pus uncore.

IX

Mult fu lét Karles de cele grant bealté:
Vit de cleres colurs li muster peinturez,
125   De martirs e de virgines e de grant majestez,
E les curs de la lune e les festes anvels
E les lavacres curre e les peisons par mer.
Karles out fer le vis, si out le chef levez;
Uns Judeus i entrat ki ben l'out esgardét.
130   Cum il vit Karle, cumençat a trembler;
Tant out fer le visage ne l'osat esgarder.
A poi que il ne chet, fuant s'en est turnét
E si muntet d'elais tuz les marbrins degrez;
Vint al patriarche, prist l'en a parler:
135   'Alez, sire, al muster, pur les funz aprester;
Orendreit me frai baptizer e lever!
Duze cuntes vi ore en cel muster entrer,
Oveoc euls le trezime, unc ne vi si formét;
Par le men escientre, ço est meimes Deus.
140   Il e li duze apostle vus venent visiter.'
Quant l'ot li patriarche, si s'en vait cunreer
E out mandét ses clers en albe en la citét.
Il les feit revestir e capes afubler;
A grant procession en est al rei alét.
145   Li emperere le vit, s'est encuntre lui levét

---

112 qui   119 si a.   124 depeinturez   135 musterer
137 musterer   142 albe la   145 si est e.

The day was fine and bright, and they set up their camp
110   And come to the church, where they left their offerings.
The doughty band of men return to their camp.

VIII

The gift which Charles offered there is very fine.
He entered a church of painted marble with a vaulted ceiling,
Within it is an altar to St Paternoster.
115   Christ sang Mass there and so did the apostles.
All twelve seats remain there still:
The thirteenth stands in the centre, sealed off and enclosed.
Charles entered, with his heart filled with joy.
When he saw the seat, he makes his way towards it;
120   The emperor sat down and he rests for a while.
The twelve peers sat in the other seats, around and beside him.
No man ever sat there before and none has done so since.

IX

Charles was overjoyed by this great beauty.
He saw the church decorated with bright-coloured paintings,
125   With martyrs and virgins and figures in great majesty,
And the courses of the moon and the annual festivals,
And pictures of running water and fish swimming in the sea.
Charles' countenance was fierce and he held his head high.
A Jew entered, who had been watching closely;
130   When he saw Charles, he began to tremble.
So fierce was his countenance that he dared not look at him;
He almost falls to the ground, then he turned and fled,
And he quickly mounts all the marble steps.
He came to the patriarch, addressing him in these words:
135   'Come to the church, my lord, to prepare the font;
I shall have myself baptized and sponsored at once.
I have just seen twelve counts enter the church,
With them a thirteenth, never have I seen one so striking.
As far as I can tell, it is God himself;
140   He and the twelve apostles are coming to visit you.'
When the patriarch hears him, he goes to make himself ready,
And he summoned his priests in their albs throughout the city.
He makes them change their clothes and put on their copes.
In a great procession he made his way to the king.
145   The emperor saw him and rose to greet him,

E out trait sun capel, parfunt lui a clinét;
Vunt sei entrebaiser, nuveles demander.
E dist li patriarche: 'Dunt estes, sire, neez?
Unkes mais nen osat hoem en cest muster entrer
150   Si ne li comandai u ne li oi ruvét.'
'Sire, jo ai nun Karle, si sui de France neez.
Duze reis ai cunquis par force e par barnez;
Li trezime vois querre dunt ai oi parler.
Vinc en Jerusalem pur l'amistét de Deu,
155   La croiz e le sepulcre sui venuz aurer.'
E dist li patriarches: 'Sire, mult estes beer.
Sis as en la chaere u sist mames Deus;
Aies nun Charles Maines sur tuz reis curunez!'
E dist li emperere: 'Cin cenz merciz de Deu!
160   De voz saintes reliques, si vus plaist, me donez,
Que porterai en France qu'en voil enluminer.'
Respont li patriarches: 'A plentét en averez.
Le braz saint Simeon aparmames en averez
E le chef saint Lazare vus frai aporter,
165   Del sanc saint Estefne, ki martir fu pur Deu.'
Karlemaines l'en rent saluz e amistez.

X

E dist li patriarches: 'Ben avez espleitez
Quan Deus venistes querre; estre vus dait le melz.
Durrai vus tels reliques, meilurs n'en ad suz cel,
170   Dul sudarie Jhesu que il out en sun chef
Cum il fu al sepulcre e posét e colchét,
Quant Judeus le garderent as espees de ascer;
Al terz jur relevat, sicum il out predicét
E il vint as apostles pur euls eslecer.
175   Un des clous averez que il out en sun péd
E la sainte corone que Deus out en sun chef,
E averez le calice que il benesquid;
La esquele de argent vus durrai volenters,
Entailee est a or e a peres precioses,
180   E averez le cultel que Deus tint al manger,
De la barbe saint Pere e des chevols de sun chef.'
Karlemaines l'en rent saluz e amistez;
Tut li cors li tressalt de joie e de pitez.

146 out taat   147 Wnt entrebaiser   158 Charles sur

And he took off his hat and bowed low to him;
They embrace each other and ask for news:
The patriarch said: 'Where do you come from, my lord?
Never before has anyone dared to enter this church
150   Unless I ordered him to do so or requested it.'
'My lord, my name is Charles and I was born in France.
I have conquered twelve kings by strength and by valour;
I am going to seek out the thirteenth of whom I have heard tell.
I came to Jerusalem for the love of God;
155   I have come to worship the cross and the sepulchre.'
The patriarch replied: 'My lord, you are a man of great worth!
You sat in the seat in which God himself sat.
May your name be Charlemagne, crowned above all kings.'
The emperor said: 'A great many thanks in God's name!
160   Give me, if you please, some of your holy relics,
Which I shall take to France, as I wish to illuminate it with them.'
The patriarch replies: 'You shall have them in abundance;
You will have at once the arm of St Simeon,
And I shall have the head of St Lazarus brought to you,
165   Some of the blood of St Stephen, who was martyred in God's name.'
In return Charlemagne offers him greetings and a pledge of friendship.

X

The patriarch said: 'You acted wisely
When you came to visit God; this is to bring you much profit.
I shall give you such relics that there are none finer on earth.
170   Some of the shroud of Jesus, which he wore on his head
When he was placed and lain down in the sepulchre,
With the Jews guarding him with their swords of steel.
On the third day he rose again, as he had foretold,
And he came to the apostles to bring joy to their hearts.
175   You will have one of the nails which he had in his foot
And the holy crown which God had on his head;
And you will have the chalice which he blessed.
I shall gladly give you the silver bowl,
Inlaid with gold and with precious stones,
180   And you will have the knife which God held at the Last Supper,
Part of St Peter's beard and some of the hairs from his head.'
In return Charlemagne offers him greetings and a pledge of friendship.
His whole body has a surge of joy and compassion.

XI

Ço dist li patriarche: 'Ben vus est avenuz;
185   Par le men escientre, Deus vus i a cundust.
Durrai vus teles reliques ke frunt grant vertuz:
Del leyt sainte Marie dunt ele aleytat Jhesus
Cum fud primes en terre entre nus decendut,
De la sainte chemise que ele out revestut.'
190   Karlemaines l'en rent amistét e saluz.
Cil li fist aporter, e li reis les reçut;
Les reliques sunt forz, Deus i fait grant vertuz.
Iloc juit un contrait, set anz out ke ne se mut;
Tut li os li crussirent, li ners li sunt estendut.
195   Ore sailt en peez, unkes plus sain ne fud.
Ore veit li patriarches, Deus i fait vertut;
Tost fait le glas suner par la citét menut.
Li reis fait faire une fertere, unkes meldre ne fud,
Del plus fin or d'Arabie i out mil mars fundud.
200   Il l'a fait seiler a force e a vertuz,
A grant bendes de argent l'a fait il lier menuz;
A l'erceveske Turpin comandet que seit cundut.
Karlemaines fud lez, e tuz icil que sunt od lui.

XII

Quatre mais fud li reis en Jerusalem la vile,
205   Il e li duze par, la chere cumpanie;
Demeinent grant barnage, car li emperere est riche.
Comencent un muster ke est de sainte Marie;
Li hume de la terre la claiment la Latanie,
Car li language i venent de trestute la vile.
210   Il i vendent lur pailes, lur teiles e lur series,
Coste e canele, peivere e altres bones espices,
E maintes bones herbes que jo ne vus sai dire.
Deus est uncore el cel que en volt faire justise.

XIII

Li emperere de France i out tant demurét,
215   Li patriarche prist, si l'en ad apelét:
'Vostre cungét, bæl sire, si vus plaist, me donét;
En France a mun realme m'en estut returner.
Pos' at que jo n'i fui, si ai mult demurrét
E ne set mis barnages quel part jo sui turnét.

---

185 i acundustid (*last two letters expunged*)   203 od luile   205 e duze

XI

      The patriarch said: 'You have been most fortunate;
185   I am aware that God has brought you here.
      I shall give you such relics as will perform great miracles:
      Some of the Virgin Mary's milk, with which she suckled Jesus
      When he first came down to earth amongst us,
      And part of the holy shift which she wore.'
190   In return Charlemagne offers him greetings and a pledge of friendship.
      The patriarch had the relics brought to him and the king accepted them;
      The relics are powerful, through them God performs great miracles.
      A cripple lay there, he had not moved for seven years;
      All his bones creaked, his sinews have become taut.
195   Now he leaps to his feet, never had he been so healthy.
      Now the patriarch sees that God is performing miracles;
      At once he has the bells tolled repeatedly throughout the city.
      The king has a reliquary made, never was there one better,
      One thousand marks of purest Arabian gold had been melted for it.
200   He had it sealed tightly and firmly,
      Then bound closely with several thick bands of silver;
      He orders it to be carried to Archbishop Turpin.
      Charlemagne was filled with joy, as were all his companions.

XII

      The king was in the city of Jerusalem for four months,
205   He and the twelve peers, that worthy band of men,
      They enjoy a lavish lifestyle, for the emperor lives in splendour.
      They found a church dedicated to the Virgin Mary;
      The local inhabitants call it the Latin Church,
      For men of diverse tongues come to it from all over the city.
210   There they sell their fabrics of silk, their linen and their serge,
      Costmary and cinnamon, pepper and other fine spices,
      And many fine herbs, too numerous to mention.
      God is still in heaven and he intends to bring them to justice.

XIII

      The Emperor of France had remained there for a long time;
215   He approached the patriarch and addressed him:
      'Grant me your leave, fair lord, if you please;
      I must return to France, to my kingdom.
      It is a while since I was there and I have tarried here a long time,
      And my barons do not know where I have gone.

220 Faites .c. mulz receivere d'or e d'argent trussét.'
    E dist li patriarches: 'Ja mar en parlerez;
    Tuz li mens granz tresors vus seit abandunez.
    Tant en prengent Franceis cum en vuldrent porter,
    Mais que de Sarazins e de paiens vus gardét,
225 Qui nus volent destrure e sainte cristientez!'

XIV

    E dist li patriarches: 'Savez dunt jo vus priz?
    De Sarazins destrure ki nus ount en despit.'
    'Volenteres', ço dist Karle; sa fei si l'en plevit.

XV

    'Jo manderrai mes humes, quant que en purrai aver,
230 E irrai en Espaine, ne purat remaner.'
    Si fist il pus, car ben en gardat sa fei,
    Quant la fud mort Rollant e li .xii. per od sei.

XVI

    Li emperere de France i out tant demuréd;
    De sa muller li membret ke il oit parler.
235 Ore irrat lu rei querre que ele li out loét;
    Ja n'en prenderat mais fin tresque il averat trovét.
    La nuit le fait nuncier as Franceis as ostels;
    Cum il l'unt entendut, si orent le queres mult leez.
    Al matin par sun l'albe, quant li jurz lur apert,
240 Li mul e li sumer sunt garniz e trussét,
    E muntent li barun, el chimin sunt entrét;
    Venent en Jerico, palmes i prenent asét.
    'Utree, Deus aie!', crient e halt e cler.
    Li patriarches muntet sur un mulz sujurnez;
245 Tant cum li jurz li duret l'at cunduz e guiez.
    La nuit furent ensenble li baruns as ostels;
    Nule ren que il demandent ne lur est demurét.
    Al matin par sun l'albe, quant li jurs lur apert,
    Remuntent li barun, al chemin sunt entrét.
250 Li patriarches ad Karlemaine apelét:
    'Vostre cungé, si vus plaist, me donez.'
    E dist l'emperere: 'Al cumant Damnedeu'.
    Vunt sæi entrebaiser, atant sunt deseverét.

---

221 Ma en   222 vus seint a.   234 mendret ke il out
239 m. sun la lalbe   243 Utre

220   Accept from me a hundred mules, laden with gold and silver.'
        And the patriarch said: 'I will not hear speak of this.
        May my whole treasure be at your disposal;
        Let the Franks take as much as they can carry,
        But beware of Saracens and pagans,
225   Who are bent on destroying us and the Christian faith.'

XIV

        The patriarch said: 'Do you know what I ask of you?
        To destroy the Saracens who hold us in such contempt.'
        'Gladly', said Charles, and he gave him his word.

XV

        'I shall summon my men, as many as I can obtain,
230   And I shall go to Spain, there will be no delay.'
        This he later did, for he kept his promise well,
        When Roland was killed there and the twelve peers with him.

XVI

        The Emperor of France had remained there a long while;
        He remembers his wife and the words he had heard her speak.
235   Now he will go and seek out the king whom she had praised to him;
        He will never rest until he has found him.
        That night he announces this to his Franks in their lodgings;
        When they heard him, their hearts were filled with joy.
        In the morning, at the crack of dawn, when the daylight appears,
240   The mules and the packhorses are prepared and loaded up,
        And the barons mount, they began their journey.
        They come to Jericho and up take palm branches in abundance:
        'Onward with God's help', they cry loud and clear.
        The patriarch mounts a well-rested mule;
245   As long as daylight lasts, he led and guided Charles.
        That night the barons were together in their lodgings;
        Nothing they ask for was slow in coming.
        In the morning, at the crack of dawn, when the daylight appears,
        The barons remount, they resumed their journey.
250   The patriarch called to Charlemagne:
        'Give me leave to go, if you please.'
        And the emperor said: 'By command of the Lord God'.
        They embrace each other, then they parted.

Chevauchet li emperere od sun ruiste barnét.
255 Li reliques sunt forz, granz vertuz i fait Deus:
Que il ne venent a ewe n'en partissent les guét;
N'encuntrent aveogle ki ne seit reluminét,
Les cuntrez i redrescent e les muz funt parler.

XVII

Chevalchet li emperere od sa cumpanie grant
260 E passent montelés e les puis d'Abilant,
La Roche del Guitume e les plaines avant.
Virent Constantinoble, une citez vaillant,
Les cloches e les egles e les punz relusanz.
Destre part la citét, de une liuue grant,
265 Trovent vergers plantez de pins e de lorers beaus.
La rose i est florie, li alburs e li glazaus;
Vint mile chevalers i troverent seant
E sunt vestut de pailes e de heremins blans
E de granz peus de martre jokes as pez trainanz.
270 As eschés e as tables se vunt esbaneant
E portent lur falcuns e lur osturs asquanz,
E treis mile puceles a orfreis relusant,
Vestues sunt de pailes e ount les cors avenanz
E tenent lur amis, si se vunt deportant.
275 Atant est Karle sur un mul amblant;
A une part se turnet, si apelet Rollant:
'Ne sai ou est li reis; ici est li barnages grant'.
Un chevaler apelet, si li dist en riant:
'Amis, u est li reis? Mult le ai alee querrant.'
280 E icil li ad dist: 'Ore chevalchét avant;
A cele paile tendue verrez lu rei seant'.
Chevalchet li emperere, ne se vait atargeant;
Truvat lu rei Hugun a sa carue arant:
Les cunjungles en sunt a or fin relusant,
285 Li essués e les roes e li cultres arant.
Il ne vait mie a pét, le aguilun en sa main,
Mais de chascune part at un fort mul amblant.
Une caiere le sustent d'or suzpendant;
La sist l'emperere sur un cuisin vaillant,
290 La plume est de oriol, la teie d'escarimant,
A ses pez un escamel neelé de argent blanc,
Sun capel en sun chef, mult par sunt bel li gaunt;
Quatre estaches entur lui en estant:
Desus ad jetét un bon paile grizain.

263 e p. le lusanz   284 cuningles   287 part un f.   288 sus le tent dor

The emperor rides on with his hardy barons.
255   The relics are powerful, through them God performs great miracles;
They have only to come to water for the fords to open up;
They do not meet a blind person without his sight being restored.
The lame walk again and they make the dumb speak.

XVII

On rides the emperor with his great band of men;
260   And they cross mountains and the hills of Abilant;
They pass the Rock of Guitume and the plains farther on.
They saw Constantinople, a splendid city,
Its gleaming bells, its eagles and its bridges.
On the right of the city, for an entire league,
265   They find orchards planted with pine trees and fine laurels.
Roses, laburnum and iris are in bloom;
They found twenty thousand knights seated there,
Dressed in silken cloaks and white ermine,
And they have great marten furs reaching down to their feet.
270   They are playing chess and backgammon to pass the time
And some have with them their falcons and their hawks.
And three thousand maidens are there, in shimmering orphrey gowns,
Clad in silken cloaks and attractive in body,
And they hold their lovers and stroll about with great enjoyment.
275   Here comes Charles arriving on an ambling mule.
He turns to one side and addresses Roland:
'I do not know where the king is: but what a noble group of barons!'
He calls to a knight, saying to him with a smile:
'Friend, where is the king? I have been seeking him for a long time.'
280   And he said to him: 'Ride on then;
You will see the king sitting beneath that canopy of silk.
The emperor rides on, he does not delay;
He found King Hugo at his plough.
The yokes are of pure, shining gold,
285   As are the axles, the wheels and the cutting blades.
The king, his goad in his hand, is not on foot,
But on each side he has a strong, ambling mule.
A chair of gold, suspended in the air, supports him;
There sat the emperor on a splendid cushion,
290   Its down is made from the golden oriole, its cover from Persian silk;
At his feet is a stool inlaid with white silver,
On his head he has a hat, very fine are his gloves.
Four posts are fixed around him,
And draped over them is a fine piece of grey silk.

295   Une verge d'or fin tint li reis en sa main,
       Si a cundut sun arét tant adreceement,
       Si fait dreite sa rei cum line que tent.
       Atant est vus Carlun sur un mul amblant!

XVIII

       Li reis tint sa carue pur sun jur espleiter
300   E vint i Carlemaines tut un antif senter,
       Vit le paile tendud e le or reflambier;
       Lu rei Hugun salua, le Fort, tres volenters.
       Li reis Hugun regardet Carle, veit le cuntenant fer;
       Les braz ad gros e quarrez, le cors greile e delgét:
305   'Sire, Deus vus garise! De quei me cunusét?'
       Respont li emperere: 'Jo sui de France nét;
       Jo ai a nun Carlemaines, Rolland si est mis nes;
       Venc de Jerusalem, si m'en voil retorner,
       Vus e vostre barnage voil veer volenters.'
310   E dist Hugun li Forz: 'Ben ad set anz e melz
       Qu'en ai oi parler estrange soldeers,
       Ke si grant barnages ait nul rei suz cel.
       Un an vus retenderai, si estre i volez;
       Tant vus durrai or e argent e aveir trussez;
315   Tant en porterunt Franceis cum il en voderunt charger!
       Ore dejundrai mes beos pur la vostre amistét.'

XIX

       Li reis desjunt ses beos e laset sa carue,
       E paissent par ces præz, amunt par ces cultures.
       Li reis muntet al mul si s'en vait l'amblure.
320   'Sire', dist li reis Carle, 'ceste vostre carue,
       Tant i at de fin or que jo ne sai mesure.
       Si senz garde remaint, jo creim que ele soit perdue.'
       E dist Hugun li reis: 'De tut iceo n'aez cure;
       Unkes ne out larun tant cum ma terre dure.
325   Set anz i purrat estre, ne serrat remue.'
       Dist Willemes de Orenge: 'Sainz Pere, aiude!
       Car la tenise en France e Berteram si i fusset,
       A peals e a marteals sereit esconsue.'
       Il brochet le mul, si s'en vait l'amblure,
330   E vint sus al paleis u out sa muiller veue.
       Il la fet cunreer e cele est revestue;
       Le paleis e la sale de pailes purtendues.   -

---

314 truss   324 adure   328 escansue   330 E uiut

295   In his hand the king held a sceptre of pure gold;
And he drove his plough with such great skill
That his furrow is as straight as a die.
Here comes Charles arriving before him on an ambling mule.

XVIII

The king drove his plough to complete his daily task,
300   And Charles came up to him along an ancient path.
He saw the hanging canopy of silk and the shimmering gold;
He greeted King Hugo, the Strong, most warmly.
The king looks at Charles, he sees his fierce countenance;
His arms are large and solid, his body slim and well-proportioned.
305   'My lord, may God protect you; how is it that you know me?'
The emperor replies: 'I was born in France;
Charlemagne is my name, Roland is my nephew;
I have come from Jerusalem and wish to return home.
I dearly wish to meet you and your valiant knights.'
310   And Hugo the Strong said: 'It is a good seven years and more
Since I heard foreign soldiers say
That no king on earth has such valiant men as you.
I shall keep you here for a year, if you wish to stay;
I shall give you a great deal of silver, gold and other goods.
315   The Franks will take away as much as they wish to carry.
Now I shall unyoke my oxen, as a mark of friendship.'

XIX

The king unyokes his oxen and releases his plough;
The beasts graze in the meadows and up in the fields.
The king mounts his mule and sets off at an ambling pace.
320   'My lord', said King Charles, 'this plough of yours,
It has more pure gold in it than I could measure.
If it is left without a guard, I fear it may be lost.'
King Hugo said: 'Do not be concerned about this;
There has never been a thief throughout my land.
325   It could remain there for seven years without being touched.'
William of Orange said: 'St Peter save us!
For if I had it in France and Bertrand were there,
It would be broken up with pikes and hammers.'
King Hugo spurs his mule and rides away at an ambling pace,
330   And he came to the palace, where he saw his wife.
He has her make ready and she changed her clothes;
The palace and the hall are bedecked with silks.

Atant est vus Carlun od sa grant gent venue!

XX

Li emperere descent defors le marbre blanc;
335   Cez degrez de la sale vint al paleis errant.
Set mil chevalers i troverent seant,
A peliçuns ermins, bliauz escarimant.
As eschés e as tables se vunt esbaneant.
La fors sunt curuz li plusurs e asquanz,
340   Receurent les destrers e les forz mulz amblanz;
A les osteus les meinent cunreer gentement.
Charles vit le paleis e la richesce grant;
A or fin sunt les tables, les chaeres e li banc.
Li paleis fu listez de azur e avenant
345   Par cheres peintures a bestes e a serpenz,
A tutes creatures e oiseaus volanz.
Li paleis fud vout e desur cloanz
E fu fait par cumpas e serét noblement,
L'estache del miliu neelee d'argent blanc.
350   Cent coluns i ad tut de marbre en estant,
Cascune est a fin or neelee devant.
De quivre e de metal tregeté douz enfanz;
Cascun tient en sa buche un corn d'ivorie blanc.
Si galerne ist de mer, bise ne altre vent,
355   Ki ferent al paleis devers occident,
Il le funt turner e menut e suvent,
Cumme roe de char qui a tere decent;
Cil corn sunent e buglent e tunent ensement
Cumme taburs u toneires u grant cloches qui pent.
360   Li uns esgardet le altre ensement cum en riant,
Que ço vus fust viarie que tut fussent vivant.
Karles vit le paleis e la richesce grant;
La sue manantise ne priset mie un guant.
De sa mullier li memberet que manacé out tant.

XXI

365   'Seignurs', dist Carle, 'mult gent palais ad ci;
Tel nen out Alixandre ne li vielz Costantin,
Ne n'out Crisans de Rome, qui tanz honurs bastid.'
E tant cum li emperere cele parole had dit,
Devers les porz de la mer uit un vent venir:

---

333 grant uenue   337 blianz   343 tables e c.   344 auernant
358 e sunent ensement

Here comes Charles with his great band of men!

XX

The emperor dismounts away from the white marble block.
335 He came quickly up the palace steps to the hall;
They found seven thousand knights seated there,
Wearing cloaks of ermine and tunics of Persian silk.
They are enjoying games of chess and backgammon.
People in great numbers came running out;
340 They took the horses and the strong, ambling mules.
They lead them to the stables to be cared for properly.
Charles saw the palace and the great splendour;
The tables, the chairs and the benches are inlaid with pure gold.
The palace was decorated with blue edgings, and pleasing to behold,
345 With its costly paintings of beasts and serpents,
And a multitude of creatures and birds in flight.
The palace was vaulted and completely covered,
And it was constructed with skill and impressively solid;
The pillar in the centre was inlaid with white silver.
350 Standing there are a hundred columns of marble,
Each inlaid with pure gold at the front.
There was a moulded figure of two children in copper and metal,
Each carrying in its mouth a horn of white ivory.
If any winds, blowing in from the sea,
355 Strike the palace on the west side,
They make it revolve quickly and repeatedly,
Like a chariot's wheel rolling downhill.
Their horns blare and bellow and thunder,
Just like a drum, a clap of thunder or a huge, hanging bell.
360 One looks at the other as if they were smiling,
So that you would have sworn they were actually alive.
Charles saw the palace and the splendour of it;
He does not care one jot for his own possessions.
He recalls his wife whom he had threatened so much.

XXI

365 'My lords', said Charles, 'this is a very fine palace;
Neither Alexander nor Constantine of old had one like it,
Nor Crescentius of Rome, who built such great monuments.'
No sooner had the emperor spoken these words
Than he heard a wind coming from the sea ports.

370   Vint bruant al palais, de une part le acuillit;
        Cil l'a fait esmuveir e suef e serrit,
        Altresi le fait turner cum arbre de mulin.
        E celes imagines cornent, l'une a l'altre surrist,
        Que ceo vus fust viarie que il fussent tuz vis.
375   L'un halt, li altre cler, mult feit bel a oir;
        Ceo est avis, qui l'ascute, qu'il seit en parais,
        La u li angle chantent suef e seriz.
        Mult fud grand li orages, la neif e li gresilz,
        E li vent durs e forz, qui tant bruit e fremist.
380   Les fenestres en sunt a cristal gentilz,
        Tailees e cunfites a brames utremarin.
        Laenz fait itant requeit e suef e serit
        Cumme en mai en estét, quant soleil esclarist.
        Mult fut grés li orages e hidus e costis.
385   Karles vit le paleis turner e fremir;
        Il ne sout que ceo fud, ne l'out de luign apris.
        Ne pout ester sur pez, sur le marbre s'asist.
        Franceis sunt tuz versét, ne se poent tenir,
        E coverirent lur chés e adenz e suvin,
390   E dist li uns a l'altre: 'Mal sumes entrepris;
        Les portes sunt uvertes, si n'en poum issir.'

                           XXII

        Carles vit le palais menument turner;
        Franceis covrent lur chés, ne l'osænt esgarder.
        Li reis Hugun li Forz en est avant alez
395   E ad dit a Franceis: 'Ne vus descunfortez!'
        'Sire', dist Carlemaines, 'ne serrat ja mes el?'
        E dist Hugun li Forz: 'Un petit m'atendét'.
        Li vespere aprocet, li orages remist;
        Franceis saillent en pez; tut fu prest li supers.
400   Carles s'asist e sis ruiste barnez,
        Li reis Hugun li Forz e sa muiller delez,
        Sa fille od le crin bloi que ad le vis bel e cler,
        E out la char tant blanche cumme flur en estéd.
        Oliver l'esgardet, si la prist a amer:
405   'Plust al rei de Glorie, de saincte majestét,
        Que la tenise en France u a Dun la citét,
        Kar jo en freie pus tutes mes voluntez!'
        Entre ses denz le dist que hon nel pot escuter.
        Nule rein que il demandent ne lur fud deveez;

371 suef e e s.   379 e fefreit   381 braines   393 osæut
396 carlem serrat   401 Hugun l forz   407 ka io

370   It swept noisily up to the palace, striking it on one side,
          And causing it to move gently and smoothly;
          It makes it revolve just like the shaft of a windmill.
          And the statues blow their horns and smile at each other
          So that you would have sworn they were actually alive.
375   One was loud and the other clear, it is wonderful to hear;
          Those who hear it think they are in paradise
          Where angels sing sweetly and gently.
          The storm was tremendous, with snow and hail,
          And the wind, strong and violent, causes great noise and clatter.
380   The windows are of fine crystal,
          Cut and fashioned with ultramarine quartz.
          Inside all is then calm and tranquillity,
          As in the summer month of May when the sun is shining.
          The storm was violent, fearsome and overpowering.
385   Charles saw the palace revolve and shake;
          He did not know what it was and had never known anything like it.
          He was unable to stand upright, so he sat down on the marble floor.
          The Franks have all been sent tumbling, they cannot stand up,
          And they covered their heads, some face down, others on their backs,
390   And they said to each other: 'We're well and truly caught!
          The doors are open, yet we cannot get out of here.'

XXII

          Charles saw the palace revolving repeatedly;
          The Franks cover their heads and do not dare to look.
          King Hugo the Strong came forward
395   And said to the Franks: 'Do not be disheartened'.
          'My lord', said Charlemagne, 'will this go on for ever?'
          And Hugo the Strong said: 'Just be patient with me'.
          The evening draws close, the storm abates;
          The Franks jump to their feet, the meal was ready.
400   Charles took his seat with his hardy barons.
          King Hugo the Strong was there, and beside him his wife
          And his blond-haired daughter, whose face was beautiful and radiant,
          And whose skin was as fair as a summer flower.
          Oliver gazes at her and began to fall in love with her:
405   'Would to Almighty God in his Holy Majesty
          That I could hold her, in France or in the city of Dun,
          For then I would have my way with her!'
          He muttered these words so that he would not be overheard.
          Nothing they ask for was denied them;

410   Asez unt venesun de cerfs e de sengler
       E unt grues e gauntes e pouns enpeverez.
       A espandant lur portent le vin e le clarez,
       E cantent e vielent e rotent cil juglur.
       Franceis se desportent par grant noblitét.

XXIII

415   Cume il ourent enz al palais real mangét,
       E unt traites les napes li maistre senescal,
       Saillent li esquier en renc de tute parz:
       Il vunt as osteus cunreer lur chevaus.
       Li reis Hugun li Forz Carlemain apelat,
420   Lui e les duzce pers, sis trait a une part.
       Le rei tint par la main, en sa cambre les menat,
       Voltue, peinte a flurs, e a peres de cristal.
       Une escarbuncle i luist e cler reflambeat,
       Confite en une estache del tens le rei Golias.
425   Duze liz i ad dous, de quivre e de metal,
       Oreillers de velus e linçous de cendal;
       Al menur a traire .xx. beos e quatre cars.
       Li trezimes enmi est taillez a cumpas;
       Li pecul sunt de argent e l'espunde d'esmal.
430   Li cuvertures fud bons que Maseuz uverat,
       Une fee mult gente que li reis dunat;
       Melz en vaut li cunreiz del tresor l'Amiral.
       Ben deit li reis amer qui li abandunat
       E tant ben servit e gent le cunreat.

XXIV

435   Franceis sunt en la cambre, si unt veud les liz;
       Casqun des duze peres i ad ja le son pris.
       Li reis Hugun li Forz lur fait porter le vin;
       Sages fud e membrez, plains de maleviz.
       En la cambre, desuz un perun marbrin
440   Desuz cavez, si ad un hume mis;
       Tute la nuit les gardet par un pertus petit.
       Li carbuncles art que bien i poet home veer,
       Cume en mai en estét quant soleil esclarcist.
       Li reis Hugun li Forz a sa muiller en vint
445   E Carlemaine e Franceis se cuchent a leisir;
       Des ore gabberent li cunte e li marchis.

---

412 As pandant ur p.   422 Voltrue peint a.   423 cler e r.   426 Oreillers e v.
428 en mi etaillez   432 la amiral   444 e vint

410 They have venison and boar's meat in abundance,
And cranes, geese and peppered peacocks.
The wine and the claret flow freely,
And the jongleurs sing and play their vielles and their rotes.
The Franks enjoy themselves in very noble fashion.

XXIII

415 When they had eaten within the royal palace,
And the chief seneschals had removed the cloths from the tables,
On all sides the squires jump up one after the other.
They go to the stables to tend to the horses.
King Hugo the Strong called to Charlemagne,
420 To him and the twelve peers, and he draws them to one side.
He took the king by the hand and led them all to his chamber,
Vaulted, painted with flowers and decorated with stones of crystal.
A carbuncle glowed there and gave out a bright light,
It had been set in a column from the time of King Goliath.
425 Twelve soft beds stand there, made of copper and metal,
With pillows of velvet and silken sheets.
To move the smallest would require at least twenty oxen and four carts.
The thirteenth in the middle is skilfully wrought;
Its feet are of silver and its edges of enamel.
430 The coverlet was well made, which Maseuz fashioned,
A most noble fairy, who gave it to the king.
This adornment is worth more than the Emir's treasure;
The king should love the person who made him a gift of it
And who served him so well and equipped him so nobly.

XXIV

435 The Franks are in the chamber and they have seen the beds;
Each of the twelve peers has soon chosen his own.
King Hugo the Strong has wine brought to them.
He was wise, clever and full of cunning;
In the chamber, beneath a marble slab,
440 Hollowed out underneath, he placed one of his men;
All night long he watches them through a tiny hole.
The carbuncle burns brightly enough to give him a good view,
As on a summer's day in May, when the sun is shining.
King Hugo the Strong came to his wife,
445 And Charlemagne and the Franks retire to bed at their ease.
Then the counts and the marquises exchanged jests.

Franceis furent as cambres, si unt beuz des vins.

XXV

E dist li un a l'altre: 'Veez cum grant bealtét!
Veez cum gent palais e cum forz richetét!
450 Plust al rei de Glorie, de sainte majestét,
Carlemaine, mi sire, le oust recatét
U cunquis par ses armes en bataile champel.'
E dist Carlemaines: 'Ben dei avant gabber.
Li reis Hugun li Forz nen ad nul bacheler,
455 De tute sa mainé, qui tant seit fort membré,
Ait vestu dous haubers e dous hames fermeet,
Si seit sur un destrer curant, sujurnét.
Li reis me prestet sa espee al poin d'or adubét,
Si ferrai sur les heaumes u il erent plus chers,
460 Trancherai les haubercs e les heaumes gemmez,
Le feutre od la sele del destrer sujurnez,
Le branc ferrai en terre si jo le lés aler,
Ja nen ert mes receuz par nul hume charnel
Tresque il seit pleine haunste de terre desterét.'
465 'Par Deu', ço dist l'eschut, 'fort estes e membrét!
Refols fud li reis Hugun quant vus prestat ostel.
Si anuit meis vus oi de folie parler,
Al matin par sun l'albe vus frai cungeer.'

XXVI

E dist l'emperere: 'Gabbez, bel neis Rolland!'
470 'Volenteres, sire, tut al vostre comand.
Dites al rei Hugun qui il me prestet sun olivant,
Pus si m'en irrai la fors en cel plain:
Tant par ert fort ma aleine e li venz si bruant
Qu'en tute la cité, que si est ample e grant,
475 N'i remaindrat ja porte ne postits en astant,
Ne quivre ne acer tant seit fort ne pesant,
Ke le un ne ferge a l'altre par le vent qui ert si bruant.
Mult ert forz li reis Hugun, si il se metet en avant,
Ke il ne perde de la barbe les gernuns en brulant
480 E les granz peaus de martre qui il ad al col en turnant,
Le peliçun de ermin del dos en reversant.'
'Par Deu', ço dist li eschut, 'ci ad mal gabement!
Que fouls fist li reis Hugun que il herbegat tel gent.'

---

462 b. en terre   474 Que tute   476 quiuee

The Franks were in their chamber and they have drunk wine.

XXV

They said to each other: 'Just look at this great beauty!
Look at this fine palace and at this great splendour!
450   Would to the King of Glory, in Holy Majesty,
That Charlemagne, my lord, had bought it
Or conquered it by arms in pitched battle.'
Charlemagne said: 'I must be the first to jest.
King Hugo the Strong has no young knight
455   In his entire household, however valiant he may be,
Who, even if he is equipped with two hauberks and two helmets,
And sitting on a swift, fresh horse,
If the king lends me his sword with the pommel adorned with gold,
Could stop me striking him on his helmets' most precious points,
460   And cleaving through the hauberks and the gem-studded helmets,
The felt and the saddle on the fresh horse.
I shall drive the sword into the ground, if I let go,
So that it cannot ever be pulled out by a living soul,
Until a full lance's length of earth has been dug up.'
465   'In God's name', said the spy, 'you are strong and valiant!
King Hugo was foolish when he granted you lodging.
If I hear any more foolish words from you tonight,
Tomorrow at daybreak I shall have you sent packing.'

XXVI

The emperor said: 'Jest, fair nephew Roland'.
470   'Willingly, my lord, just as you command.
Tell King Hugo to lend me his olifant;
Then I shall go forth on to the plain.
So powerful will be my breath and the wind so violent
That throughout the whole of this city, which is so large and spacious,
475   No door or postern will remain standing,
And copper and steel, however strong and heavy,
Will come crashing together in the blustery wind.
King Hugo will be very strong if he ventures forth
And does not have his whiskers burnt off his beard
480   And his great marten skins whisked away from his neck,
His ermine cloak turned inside out on his back.'
'In God's name', said the spy, 'this is a bad jest!
What a fool King Hugo was to give lodging to such men.'

XXVII

'Gabbez, sire Oliver', dist Rolland li curteis.
485 'Volenteres', dist li quens, 'mais Carlemaine le otrait!
Prenget li reis sa fille, qui tant ad bloi le peil,
En sa cambre nus metet en un lit en requeit;
Si jo ne l'ai anut, testimonie de lui, cent feiz,
Demain perde la teste, par covent le otrai.'
490 'Par Deu', ço dist li eschut, 'vus recrerez anceis!
Grant huntage avez dit, mais quel sacet li reis,
En trestute sa vie mes ne vus amereit.'

XXVIII

'E vus, sire arcevesque, gaberez vus od nus?'
'Oil', ço dist Turpin, 'par le comant Carlun.
495 Treis des meillurs destrers que en sa cité sunt
Prenget li reis demain, si en facet faire un curs!
La defors en cel plain, quant melz s'esleserunt,
Jo venderai sur destre curant par tel vigur
Que me serrai al terz, si larrai les deus;
500 E tendrai quatre pumes mult grosses en mun puin,
Sis irrai estruant e getant cuntremunt,
E lerrai les destrers aler a lur bandun;
Se pume m'en escapet, ne altre en chet del poin,
Carlemain mi sire me crevet les oilz del frunt!'
505 'Par Deu', ço dist li escut, 'cist gas est bel e bon!
Vers mun seignur lu rei n'i had huntage nul.'

XXIX

Dist Willelmes de Orenge: 'Seignurs, ore gaberai.
Veez cele grant pelote? Unc grainur ne vi meis;
Entre or fin e argent gardét cumben i ad!
510 Meinte feiz i sunt mis .xxx. humes en assai,
Ne la poreint muer, tant fud pesant li fais.
A une sule main par matin la prendrai,
Puis la larrai aler tres parmi cel palais,
Mais de quarante teises del mur en abaterai.'
515 'Par Deu', ço dist li escut, 'ja ne vus en crerai!
Trestut sait fel li reis si asaier ne vus fait!
Ainz que seiez calcét, le matin le dirrai.'

---

490 uus uus r.   491 que il sacet   495 des desmeillurs   499 Qui me

XXVII

'Jest, Lord Oliver', said Roland the courtly.
485 'Willingly', said the count, 'with Charlemagne's permission.
Let the king take his daughter, whose hair is so fair,
And place us in the same bed together in her chamber.
If on her admission I don't take her one hundred times in the night,
May I lose my head tomorrow, on this I give my word.'
490 'In God's name', said the spy, 'you will give up before then!
Your words are most shameful, and should the king know of this,
As long as he lives, he would never love you.'

XXVIII

'And you, Lord Archbishop, will you jest with us?'
'Yes', said Turpin, 'if Charles commands it.
495 Tomorrow let the king take three of the finest horses,
Which there are in the city, and make a track for them.
Out there on the plain, when they are at full gallop,
I shall come running from the right with such strength
That I shall get astride the third horse and let the other two go.
500 And I shall hold in my hand four huge apples,
Come riding along, tossing them and throwing them up,
And give the horses free rein:
If I fail to catch any apple, or else drop one,
Let my lord Charlemagne pluck the eyes from my head.'
505 'In God's name', said the spy, 'this is a fine and handsome jest!
There is no shame to my lord in this.'

XXIX

William of Orange said: 'My lords, now I shall jest.
Do you see that great sphere? I have never seen one larger.
Look how much pure gold and silver it contains!
510 Many a time thirty men have been put to the test,
But they could not move it, so great was its weight.
Tomorrow morning I shall take it in one hand,
Then I shall let it roll right through the middle of the palace
And knock down more than forty yards of wall.'
515 'In God's name', said the spy, 'I shall never believe you!
Shame on the king if he does not put you to the test.
First thing in the morning, before you are dressed, I shall tell him.'

XXX

E dist li emperere: 'Ore gaberat Ogers,
Li dux de Denemarche, qui tant se put traveiller.'
520 'Volenteres', dist li bers, 'tut al vostre cungiét.
Veez vus cele estache que le palais sustent,
Que ui matin veistes si menut turner?
Demain la me verrét par vertut embracer,
Ne ert tant fort le estache ke ne l'estucet briser
525 E le palais verser, vers terre trubucer.
Ki la ert acunseuz, ja garantiz nen ert;
Mult ert fous li reis si il ne se vait mucer.'
'Par Deu', ço dist li eschut, 'cist home est enragez!
Unques Deus ne vus duinst cel gab cumencer,
530 Que fols fist li reis qui vus ad herbergét!'

XXXI

E dist li emperere: 'Gabez, Naimes li dux!
'Volenteres', dist li bers; 'tut le peil ai canut.
Dites al rei Hugun qui il me prest sun hoberc brun;
Demain, quant jo l'averai endossét e vestut,
535 Me verrés escure par force a tel vertuz,
N'ert tant fort li hobercs d'acer ne blanc ne brun
Que n'en cheent les mailles ensement cumme festuz.'
'Par Deu', ço dist l'escut, 'veilz estes e canuz!
Tut avez le peil blanc, mult avez les ners durs!'

XXXII

540 E dist li empereres: 'Gabez, dan Berenger!'
'Volenters', dist li quens, 'quant vus le comandez.
Prenget li reis espees de tuz les chevalers,
Facet les enterer entreque as helz d'or mer
Que les pointes en seient cuntremunt vers le cel!
545 En la plus halte tur m'en munterai a pét
E pus sur les espees m'en larai derocher.
La verrez brans crussir e espees brisier,
L'un acer a l'altre depecer e entreoscher;
Ja ne troverez une qui m'at en char tuchét,
550 Ne le quir entamét ne en parfunt plaét.'
'Par Deu', ço dist l'eschut, 'cist hon est enragét!
Si il cel gabs demustre, de fer est u d'acer!'

---

522 veistis   534 Demait   538 ueilz est   543 entreque haltes   544 seint
548 de peces

XXX

The emperor said: 'Now Ogier will jest,
The Duke of Denmark, who never shirks hard work.'
520   'Willingly', said the baron, 'with your permission.
Do you see that column, which supports the palace
Which this morning you saw rotating repeatedly?
Tomorrow you will see me grasp the column with such strength
That, however strong it is, it will have to break
525   And the palace topple and come tumbling down.
Anyone caught unawares will have no protection.
The king will be a fool if he does not go and take cover.'
'In God's name', said the spy, 'this man is mad!
May God never permit him to undertake this jest;
530   What a fool the king was who has given you lodging.'

XXXI

The emperor said: 'Jest, Duke Naimes'.
'Willingly', said the baron. 'All my hair is white;
Tell King Hugo to lend me his burnished hauberk.
Tomorrow, when I have put it on and dressed in it,
535   You will see me shake myself with such strength and force
That, however strong the hauberk, of white or burnished steel,
Nothing will prevent its links from falling away like corn-stalks.'
'In God's name', said the spy, 'you are old and white-haired!
Your hair may well be white, but you have very tough sinews.'

XXXII

540   The emperor said: 'Jest, Lord Berenger'.
'Willingly', said the count, now that you order me to.
Let the king take swords from all his knights
And have them buried up to their pure gold hilts
So that the points stick up towards the sky.
545   I shall walk up to the top of the tallest tower
And then let myself fall on to the swords.
Then you will see blades crunching and swords breaking,
Steel shattering on steel and flying into pieces;
You will not find a single one which has harmed me,
550   Scratched my skin or caused a deep wound.'
'In God's name', said the spy, 'this man is mad!
If he accomplishes this jest, he is made of iron or steel!'

XXXIII

E dist li empereres: 'Sire Bernard, gabez'.
'Volenters', dist li quens, 'quant vus le cummandez.
555   Veistes cele grant ewe qui si brut a cel guét?
Demain la frai tute issir de sun canel,
Aspandre par ces camps, que vus tuz le verrez,
Tuz les celers aemplir que sunt en la citez,
La gent lu rei Hugun moillir e guaer,
560   En la plus halte tur lui maimes munter;
Ja n'en descendrat si l'averai comandét.'
'Par Deu', ço dist l'eschut, 'cist hon est enragét!
Que fols fist li reis Hugue qui vus prestat ostel!
Le matin par sun l'albe serrez tuz cungeez!'

XXXIV

565   E dist li quens Bertram: 'Or gaberat mis uncles'.
'Volenters, par ma fei', dist Ernalz de Girunde.
Ore prenget li reis Hugue de plum quatre sumes,
Sis facet en calderes tutes ensemble fundre,
E prenget une cuve que seit grande e parfunde,
570   Si la facet raser desque as espondes;
Pus me serrai enmi tresque la basse nune.
Quant li pluns iert tuz pris e rasises les undes,
Cum il ert ben serrez, dunc me verrez escure
E le plum departir e desur mei desrumpre;
575   Nen i remandrat ja pesant une escalunie.'
'Ci ad merveillus gab!', ceo ad dist li escut.
'Unc de si dure carn n'oi parler sur hume;
De fer est u d'acer si cest gab demustret.'

XXXV

Ço dist li emperere: 'Gabez, sire Aimer'.
580   'Volenters', dist li quens, 'quant le comandét.
Uncore ai un capel, de almande engulét,
D'un grant peisun marage que fud fait en mer;
Quant l'avrai en mun chef vestud e afublét,
Demain quant li reis Hugue serrat a sun deigner,
585   Mangerai sun peisun e bevrai sun clarét;
Puis viendrai par detrés, durrai lui un cop tel

---

563 prstat   565 Bertraam   571 b. nuue   575 i ia p. un es scalume
582 p. mage;   fait sur (*expunged*) en mer

XXXIII

The emperor said: 'Lord Bernard, jest'.
'Willingly', said the count, 'now that you order me to.
555   Did you see that great river which roars so loudly at the ford?
Tomorrow I shall make it leave its bed completely
And flow over the fields in full sight of everyone;
All the cellars in the city will be filled
And King Hugo's men will be soaked and wet through,
560   He himself will climb to the highest tower
And not come down until I give the order.'
'In God's name', said the spy, 'this man is mad!
What a fool King Hugo was to give you lodging!
In the morning, at the crack of dawn, you will all be sent packing.'

XXXIV

565   Count Bertrand said: 'Now my uncle will jest'.
'Willingly, by my faith', said Ernaut de Gironde.
'Now let King Hugo take four loads of lead,
Melt them all down together in cauldrons
And take a vat which is large and deep,
570   And have it filled right up to the brim;
Then I shall sit in the middle of it until late afternoon.
When the lead has completely set and stopped bubbling,
As soon as it is really firm, you will then see me shake myself down
And split the lead and break it loose from under me;
575   Not even a shallot's weight will be left on it.'
'This is a wondrous jest!' said the spy,
'I have never heard of any man with such tough skin;
He is made of iron or steel, if he accomplishes this jest.'

XXXV

The emperor said: 'Jest, Lord Aimer'.
580   'Willingly', said the count, 'now that you order me to.
I have a hat, trimmed with almandine
And made at sea from the skin of a great sea creature.
When I have put it on and am wearing it,
Tomorrow, when King Hugo is seated at dinner,
585   I shall eat his fish and drink his claret;
Then I shall come up behind him and give him such a blow

Que devant sur sa table le frai encliner.
La verrez barbes traire e gernuns si peler!'
'Par Deu', ço dist li escut, 'cist hon est enragét!
590   Que fols fist li reis Hugue qui vus prestat ostel.'

XXXVI

'Gabez, sire Bertram!' li emperere ad dit.
'Volenters', dist li quens, 'tut al vostre plaisir.
Treis escuz forz e roiz m'empruntez le matin,
Puis m'en irrai la fors en sunz cel pin antif.
595   La les me verrez ensemble par tel vertud ferir
E voler cuntremunt; si m'escrierai si
Que en quatre liues envirun le pais
Ne remandrat en bois cerf ne daim a fuir,
Nule bise salvage ne cheverol ne gupil.'
600   'Par Deu', ço dist li escut, 'mal gabement ad ci!
Quant le saverat li reis Hugue, grains ert e maris.

XXXVII

'Gabez, sire Genin!' dist l'emperere Carles.
'Volenters', dist li quens. 'Demain, veant les altres,
Un espeed fort e roist m'aportez en la place,
605   Que grant seit e pesant, uns vilains i at carges,
Li haunste de pomer, de fer i ait un alne;
En sumét cele tur, sur cel piler de marbre,
Me culchez dous deners, que li uns seit sur l'altre;
Puis m'en istrai ensus de une liue large,
610   Si me verrez lancer, si vus en pernez garde,
Tresque al piét de la tur lu un deners abatre,
Si suef e serid, ja nes muera li altre.
Puis serrai si legers e ignals e ates
Que m'en vendrai curant parmi le us de la sale
615   E reprendrai l'espeet ainz qu'a tere s'abaiset.'
'Par Deu', ço dist l'escut, 'cist gab valt .iii. des altres!
Vers mun seignur lu rei n'i ad gens de huntage.'

XXXVIII

Quant li cunte unt gabét, si s'en sunt endormit.
Li eschut ist de cambre que trestut ad oit;
620   Vint a l'us de la cambre u li reis Hugue gist,

---

591 Bertraram   593 memprutez   609 mensterrai   612 et tercid
615 E repundrai

That I shall lay him out on the table in front of him.
Then you will see beards pulled and whiskers torn off!'
'In God's name', said the spy, 'this mad is mad!
590   What a fool King Hugo was to give you lodging.'

XXXVI

'Jest, Lord Bertrand', said the emperor.
'Willingly', said the count, 'just as you wish.
Get me three strong and sturdy shields tomorrow morning,
Then I shall go up to the top of that ancient pine outside,
595   And there you will see me strike them together so forcibly
And go flying through the air, shouting so loudly
That for four leagues around this place
No stag or buck will fail to flee from the wood,
No woodland hind, no roe and no fox.'
600   'In God's name', said the spy, 'this is a bad jest!
When King Hugo hears of it, he will be vexed and distressed.'

XXXVII

'Jest, Lord Genin', said the Emperor Charles.
'Willingly', said the count. 'Tomorrow, in everyone's sight,
Bring out here a strong and sturdy spear;
605   Make it big and heavy, such that a peasant would find it weighty.
Let it have a shaft of apple wood and an iron tip four feet long.
At the top of that tower, on the marble pillar,
Place two coins for me, one on top of the other;
Then I shall withdraw more than a full league;
610   And you will see me rush, if you watch carefully,
Right up to the foot of the tower, throw the spear and dislodge
One of the coins smoothly and cleanly, without moving the other.
Then I shall be so sprightly, speedy and nimble
That I shall come racing through the door of the hall
615   And catch the spear before it lands on the ground.'
'In God's name', said the spy, 'this jest is worth three of the others!
It causes no shame at all to my lord the king.'

XXXVIII

When the counts have jested, they fell asleep.
The spy, who has heard everything, leaves the chamber.
620   He came to the door of the chamber where King Hugo was asleep;

Entreuvert l'ad trovéd, si s'en est venuz al lit.
Li emperere le vit, hastivement li dist:
'Diva! Que funt Franceis e Karles od le fer vis?
Ois les parler s'il remandrunt a mi?'
625   'Par Deu', ço dist li escut, 'unc ne lur en suvint;
Asez vus unt anut gabét e ascarnit.'
Tuz les gas cuntat, quanc que il en oid.
Quant l'entent le reis Hugue, grains en fud e mariz.

XXXIX

'Par ma fei', dist li reis, 'Carles ad feit folie
630   Quant il gaba de moi par si grant legerie.
Herberjai les ersair en mes cambres perines;
Si ne sunt aampli li gab sicum il les distrent,
Trancherai lur les testes od ma spee furbie!'
E mandet de ses humes en avant de cent mile;
635   Il lur ad cumandét que aient vestu brunies
E capes afublez e ceintes espees burnies.
Il entrent al palais, entur lui s'asistrent.
Karle vint de muster quant la messe fu dite,
Il e li duze per, les feres cumpainies.
640   Devant vait li emperere, car il est li plus riches,
E portet en sa main un ramisel de olive.
Li reis Hugue le vit, de luinz le cuntraliet:
'Carles, purquei gabastes de moi e escarnites?
Ersair vus herberjai en mes cambres perines;
645   Nel dusez ja penser par si grant legerie!
Si ore ne sunt aampli li gab que vus deistes,
Trancherai vus les testes od ma spee furbie!'
Quant l'entent l'emperere, si se creinst de sa vie,
E regardet Franceis, les feres compaignies:
650   'Del vin e del clarét fumes ersair tuz ivres;
Jo quid qui li reis out en sa cambre s'espie.'

XL

'Sire', dist Carlemaine, 'ersair nus herbergastes;
Del vin e de el asez nus en donastes.
Si est tel custume en France, a Paris e a Cartres,
655   Quant Franceis sunt culchiez, que se guiunt e gabent
E si dient ambure e saver e folage.
Ore me lesez parler a mun ruiste barnage,

---

623 que sunt f.   624 remaindrum   627 Tuz les cuntat   629 perar
ma f.   634 cennt   636 espeea   645 pa   648 de sai v.   649 compaigines

He found it ajar and he came up to the bed.
The emperor saw him and said to him at once:
'Come! What are the Franks doing, and Charles with the fierce glance?
Did you hear them say whether they will remain faithful to me?'
625 'In God's name', said the spy, 'it never crossed their minds;
This night they mocked and scorned you a great deal.'
He related all the jests, as many as he had heard.
When King Hugo hears him, he was vexed and distressed.

XXXIX

'Upon my word', said the king, 'Charles has acted foolishly
630 When he jested so recklessly at my expense.
This night I lodged them in my chambers of stone;
If the jests are not accomplished just as they were uttered,
I shall cut off their heads with my polished sword.'
And he summons more than a hundred thousand vassals;
635 He ordered them to put on their hauberks
And to don their cloaks and gird on their burnished swords.
They enter the palace and sat down around him.
Charles came from the church when the Mass was over,
He and the twelve peers, his hardy companions.
640 The emperor is out in front, for he cuts the most splendid figure of all,
And he carries in his hand a small olive branch.
King Hugo saw him, from afar he speaks angrily to him:
'Charles, why did you jest at my expense and mock me?
Last night I lodged you in my chambers of stone;
645 You ought not to have had such reckless thoughts.
If the jests which you uttered are not now accomplished,
I shall cut off your heads with my polished sword.'
When the emperor hears him, he is afraid for his life,
And he looks at the Franks, his fierce companions:
650 'Last night we were quite drunk on wine and claret;
I think that the king had a spy in his chamber.'

XL

'My lord', said Charlemagne, 'last night you lodged us;
You gave us wine and other things in abundance.
It is customary in France, in Paris or in Chartres,
655 For Franks, when they retire to bed, to sport and jest like that,
And they thus speak words which are both sensible and foolish.
Now let me speak with my mighty barons;

Si vus en responderai volenters par vionage.'
'A fei', ço dist li reis, 'trop i out grant huntage.
660 Par ma fei', ço dist Hugun, 'e par ma blanche barbe,
Quant de mei partirez, ja ne gaberét mais altre.'

XLI

Carlemaine s'en turnet e li .xii. per od lui,
E vunt en un cunseil desuz un arc volsud.
'Seignurs', dist l'emperere, 'mal nus est avenud:
665 De vin e del clarét tant eumes beud
E desimes tele chose que estre ne dust.'
E ad fait les reliques aporter devant lui.
A ureisuns se getent, si unt lur culpes batud
E prient Deu del cel e la sue vertud
670 Del rei Hugun le Fort que il les garisset ui,
Que encuntre lur est forment irascud.
Atant ast vus un angele qui Deus i aparut,
E vint a Carlemaine, si l'ad relevéd sus:
'Carlemaine, ne t'esmaer, ço te mandet Jhesus!
675 Des gas que ersair desistes, grant folie fud;
Ne gabez mes hume, ço te cumandet Cristus.
Va, si fas cumencer, ja n'en faldrat uns.'
L'emperere l'entent, leez e joiant en fud.

XLII

Carlemaine de France il fud levéd en peez,
680 E out drescé sa main, en croiz seigna sun chef,
E ad dit a Franceis: 'Pas ne vus esmaez!
Devant lu rei Hugun al palais en venez!'

XLIII

'Sire', dist Carlemaine, 'ne puis lesser nel die:
Ersair nus herberjastes en vus cambres perines,
685 Del vin e del clarét li asquanz furent iveres.
Quant de nus turnastes, grant outrage feistes:
En la cambre leisastes oveoc nus vostre espie.
Nus savum itele terre u custume est asise,
Si vus l'eusez fait, i ust felunie.
690 Nus les aamplirum, ne puet remaner mie;
Ki en avez coisit, icil comencerat primes.'
'E', dist Hugun le Fort − ne l'ad mescoisi mie −,

---

663 arc usud   673 E unt a c.   683 puus   688 sauunn

I shall gladly respond to your charge with due surety.'
'My word', said the king, 'this was a very shameful thing to do.
660 Upon my word', said King Hugo, 'and by my white beard,
When you leave me, you will never mock anyone again.'

XLI

Charlemagne departs and his twelve peers with him,
And they go to take counsel beneath a vaulted arch.
'My lords', said the emperor, 'misfortune has come upon us.
665 We had drunk so much wine and claret
That we said things which ought not to have been said.'
And he had the relics brought before him.
They prostrate themselves in prayer and confessed their sins,
And they beseech God in Heaven, in his power,
670 To save them that day from King Hugo the Strong
Who is greatly angered by them.
Then, lo, there came an angel sent by God,
And he came to Charlemagne and raised him up.
'Charlemagne, fear not, Jesus sends you this message:
675 To jest as you did last night was an act of great folly.
Never mock anyone again; this is Christ's command.
Go, let it begin, none of them will fail.'
The emperor hears him, he was happy and filled with joy.

XLII

Charlemagne of France had got to his feet,
680 And had raised his hand, crossed himself
And said to the Franks: 'Do not be afraid;
Come before King Hugo in the palace'.

XLIII

'My lord', said Charlemagne, 'I must have my say;
Last night you lodged us in your chambers of stone.
685 Some of us were drunk on wine and claret.
When you left us, you performed an outrageous act;
In the chamber you left your spy with us.
We know a land where the custom is established that,
If you had done such a thing, it would have been treachery.
690 We shall accomplish them, there can be no delay,
The man you have chosen will be the first to begin.'
'Look', said Hugo the Strong - he did not make a bad choice -

'Ci astat Oliver qui dist si grant folie,
Que en une sule nuit avereit cent feiz ma fille.
695   Fel seie en tutes curz si jo li nel delivre!
Si ne li abandun, dunc ne me pris jo mie.
Mais faille une sule feiz par sa recreantise,
Trancherai lui la teste a ma spee furbie;
Il e lé duze per sunt livréd a martirie.'
700   Carlemaine s'en rist, que en Deu s'en afied,
E dist a l'altre mot: 'Ja mar l'en larréd quite'.
Tute jur se deportent, guient e esbanient;
Nule ren que il demandent ne lur atarge mie,
Tresque il vint a la nuit que tut est aserie.
705   Li reis fait en sa cambre cunduire sa fille,
Purtendue est trestute de pailles e de curtines;
Ele out la carn tant blanche cum flur en esté.
Oliver i entrat, si començat a rire.
Quant le vit la pucele, mult est aspourie;
710   Purquant si fud curteise, gente parole ad dite:
'Sire, eissistis de France pur nus femmes ocire?'
E respund Oliver: 'Ne dutez, bele amie!
Si crere me volez, tute en serrez garie.'

XLIV

Oliver gist el lit lez la fille le rei;
715   Devers sei l'a turnét si la beisat .iii. feiz.
Ele fud ben cointe, e il dist que curteis:
'Dame, mult estes bele, car estes fille de rei.
Pureoc si dis mun gab, ja mar vus en crendrez;
De vus mes volentez aamplir, ço ne quier a veir.'
720   'Sire', dist la pucele, 'aiez merci de mei!
Jamés ne serrai lee, se vus me huniset.'
'Bele', dist Oliver, 'al vostre cumant seit!
Mais m'en cuvent que m'aquitét vers lu rei.
De vus frai ma drue, ja ne quier altre aveir.'
725   Cele fud ben curteise, si l'en plevit sa fei.
Li quens ne li fist la nuit mes que .xxx.feiz!
Al matin par sun l'albe i est venuz li reis
E apelat sa fille, si li dist en requeit:
'Dites mei, bele fille, ad le vus fait .c. feiz?'
730   Cele li respunt: 'Oïl, sire reis'.
Ne fait a demander si irascud fu li reis.
E vint al palais u Carlemaine seait.
'Li primers est gariz; encanteres est, ço crei!

---

694 que une   700 afiod   701 quite *is lacking*   715 se la

'Here stands Oliver, who said with such great folly
That in a single night he would have my daughter a hundred times.
695   May I be cursed in every court if I do not hand her over!
If I do not let him have her, then I have no regard for myself.
But if he should fail and admit defeat even once
I shall cut off his head with my polished sword;
He and the twelve peers are doomed to die.'
700   Charlemagne laughed, for he trusts in God,
And he added these words: 'It would be wrong for you to let him off'.
All day long they amuse themselves, have fun and make merry;
Nothing they ask for is slow in coming,
Until night-time arrived and darkness fell.
705   The king has his daughter taken to her chamber;
Its walls are completely covered with silks and curtains.
Her skin was as white as a summer flower.
Oliver entered and began to laugh.
When the maiden saw him, she was very much afraid;
710   Yet she was courtly, she spoke to him in noble terms:
'My lord, did you leave France in order to kill us women?'
And Oliver replies: 'Have no fear, fair one!
If you are willingly to take my word for it, you will emerge unscathed.'

XLIV

Oliver lies down in the bed beside the king's daughter;
715   He turned her towards him and kissed her three times.
She was very comely and he spoke to her in courtly fashion:
'My lady, you are very beautiful, for you are a king's daughter.
So, even if I did make my jest, you must not fear it;
I have truly no intention of accomplishing my desire with you.'
720   'My lord', said the maiden, 'have pity on me.
I shall never again know joy if you dishonour me.'
'Fair one', said Oliver, 'let it be as you wish;
But it is necessary for you to acquit me with the king.
I shall make you my sweetheart, I shall seek no other.'
725   She was very courtly and she pledged her faith.
That night the count did it to her no more than thirty times!
In the morning, at the crack of dawn, the king came
And called his daughter and said to her in private:
'Tell me, fair daughter, did he do it to you a hundred times?'
730   She replies to him: 'Yes, my lord king'.
There is no need to ask whether the king was angry.
He came to the palace where Charlemagne was seated:
'The first one is safe, I think he must be a magician;

Ore voil saveir des altres si mençunge est u veir.'

XLV

735 Dolenz fud li reis del gab que est aampliz
E dist a Carlemaine: 'Li primers est gariz,
E voil saveir des altres s'il ferunt altresi'.
'Cil comencerat ki en avez coisit.'
'La veez ci Willeme, filz le cunte Ameri.
740 Ore prenget la pelote ke en la cambre gist;
Se issi ne la getet cum il erseir le dist,
Trancherai lui la teste a mun brant acerin.
Il e li .xii. per sunt venuz a lur fin!'

XLVI

Ore veit li quens Guillames que li gas fud sur lui,
745 Dunc desfublet ses paus dunt li beveres fud bruns;
Par les neiles de paile les ad getét jus.
Vint errant en la cambre u la pelote fud,
A une main la levet, si la trait par vertud,
Si la lessat aler que trestut l'unt veud;
750 Mais de quarante teises ad del mur abatud.
Ne fu mie par force, mes par Deu vertud,
Pur amur Carlemaine chis i out acunduit.
Dolenz fud li reis Hugun de sun palais ki fud fenduz.

XLVII

Si ad dit a ses humes: 'Mal gabement ad ci!
755 Par la fei que vus dei, nen est bel ne gentilz;
Ces sunt ancantur qui sunt entrez ceenz.
Volent tenir ma tere e tuz mes casemenz.
Ore voil saver des altres si ferunt ensement.
Mais si un en fault, par Deu omnipotent,
760 Demain les frai pendre en sun cel pin al vent,
A unes forz estaches, nen averunt raement.'

XLVIII

'Sire', dist Carlemaines, 'volez en mes des gas?
Ki en avez coisit cil recumencerat.'
E dist Hugun li Forz: 'Veez ci Bernard,
765 Filz le cunte Aimer, ki de ço se vantat

---

745 beueris   755 que si dei   761 raidement

Now I intend to find out if the others have lied or told the truth.'

XLV

735 The king was distressed by the jest which has been accomplished,
And he said to Charlemagne: 'The first one is safe,
And I intend to find out if the others will do the same.'
'The man whom you have chosen will begin.'
'Here is William, son of Count Aimeri.
740 Let him now take the sphere which lies in the chamber,
And if he does not throw it as he said last night,
I shall cut off his head with my sword of steel.
He and the twelve peers have reached their end of their lives.'

XLVI

Now Count William sees that the jest has fallen to him,
745 So he takes off his coat of brown beaver-skin
And threw it down against the silken tapestries.
He came at once to the chamber where the sphere lay;
He picks it up in one hand and draws it back powerfully,
And he let go of it before everyone's eyes.
750 It knocked down more than forty yards of wall.
This was not through his own strength, but through the power of God,
Because of his love for Charlemagne who had brought them there.
King Hugo was distressed that his palace had been damaged.

XLVII

He said to his men: 'This is a bad jest!
755 By the faith which I owe, it is not good or worthy;
These are magicians who have come here.
They intend to take possession of my land and all my fiefs;
Now I want to find out if the others will do the same.
But if one of them fails, by Almighty God,
760 Tomorrow I shall have them hanged in the wind from that pine tree,
From a sturdy gallows, they will not redeem their lives.'

XLVIII

'My lord', said Charlemagne, 'do you want more of the jests?
The man whom you have chosen will take his turn.'
And Hugo the Strong said: 'Here is Bernard,
765 Son of Count Aimeri, whose boast it was

Que icele grant ewe, que brut a cel val,
Que il la freit eisir tute de sun canal,
Entrer en la citét, curre de tutes parz,
Mai mames munter en mun plus halt palais,
770   Que n'en purrai decendre tresque il cumandereit.'

XLIX

Ore set li quens Bernard lui estut cumencer,
E dist a Carlemaine: 'Damnedeu en priez!'
Il vent curant a l'ewe, si ad les guez seignez;
Deus i fist miracles, li Glorius de cel,
775   Que tute la grant ewe fait isir de sun biéd,
Aspandere par les camps, que tuz le virent ben,
Entrer en la citez e emplir les celers,
La gent lu rei Hugun e moiller e guaer;
En la plus halte tur li reis s'en fuid a péd.
780   Desur un pin antif est Carle al vis fer,
Il e li duze pers, li barun chevaler,
Prient Dampnedeu qui de eauls ait pitéd.

L

Desur un pin antif est Carlemaines,
Il e li duze per, lé gentes cumpaines.
785   Oit lu rei Hugun sus en la tur deplaindre:
Sun tresor li durat, sil cundurat en France
E devendrat ses homes, de lui tendrat sun regne.
Quant l'entend l'emperere, pitét en a mult grande —
Envers humilitét se deit eom ben enfraindre —
790   E priet a Jhesu que cele ewe remaignet.
Deus i fist grant vertut pur amur Carlemaigne:
L'eve ist de la citét, si s'en vait par les plaines,
Reentret en sun canal, les rives en sunt pleines.
Des or put ben li reis jus de la tur decendre,
795   E vent a Carlemaine desuz l'umbre de une ente.
'A feiz, dreiz emperere, jo sai ke Deus vus aime!
Tis hom voil devenir, de tei tendrai mun regne;
Mun tresor te durrai, sil frai amener en France.'
'Volez en mes des gas, sire?' dist Carlemaine.
800   E dist Hugun li Forz: 'Ne de ceste semaine!
Si tuz sunt aampli, ja ne ert jur ke ne me plaigne.'

766 Q. ile   776 aspandere les c.   778 lui r.   788 leperere
794 Des put   798 si f.

That the great river, which roars through the valley,
He could make leave its bed completely,
Enter the city, flow in every direction,
So that I myself would climb up to the highest point in my palace
770 And be unable to come down until he gives the order.'

XLIX

Now Count Bernard knows that he had to begin,
And he said to Charlemagne: 'Pray to the Lord God!'
He runs to the river and has blessed the fords;
God performed a miracle there, the Glorious One in Heaven,
775 So that the great river is made to leave its bed
And flow through the fields in full sight of everyone,
Enter the city and fill up the cellars,
And wet and soak King Hugo's people;
The king flees on foot to the highest tower.
780 Charles with the fierce countenance is in an ancient pine,
He and the twelve peers, the courageous knights.
They beseech the Lord God to take pity on them.

L

Charlemagne is in an ancient pine tree,
He and the twelve peers, the noble companions.
785 He heard the laments of King Hugo in the tower:
He will give him his treasure and accompany him to France,
And become his vassal and hold his kingdom from him.
When the emperor hears him, he takes great pity on him —
One should give ground in the face of humility —
790 And he prays to Jesus for the river to desist.
God performed a great miracle for love of Charlemagne:
The water leaves the city and retreats across the plains.
It returns to its bed, the banks are filled up;
Then the king could come down from the tower,
795 And he comes to Charlemagne beneath the shade of a fruit tree.
'In faith, rightful emperor, I know that God loves you!
I wish to become your vassal, I shall hold my kingdom from you.
I shall give you my treasure and have it taken to France.'
'Do you want more of the jests, my lord?' said Charlemagne.
800 And King Hugo the Strong replies: 'Not this week!
If they are all accomplished, I shall never cease to lament.'

LI

'Sire', dist Carlemaine al rei Hugun le Fort,
'Ore estes vus mis heoms veant tuz les voz.
Hui devums vus faire feste, barnage e grant deport
805   E porterum ensemble les corunes a or.
Pur la vostre amistét prest sui la meie en port.'
'E jo, sire, la meie', dist Hugun, 'al vostre los,
Si ferum processiun la dedenz cel enclos.'
Karlemaines portet la grant corone a or,
810   Li reis Hugun la sue plus basement un poi:
Karlemaines fud graindre plein péd e .iii. pouz.
Franceis les esgardent, n'i out un n'en parolt:
'Ma dame la reine dist folie e tord.
Mult par est Karlemaines ber pur demener esforz;
815   Ja ne vendrum en terre nostre ne seit li los.'

LII

Karlemaine portet corune dedenz Costentinoble,
Li reis Hugue la sue plus bassement uncore.
Franceis les esgardent, li plusur en parolent:
'Ma dame la reine, ele dist mult que fole,
820   Que preisat barnét si ben cum le nostre.'
Si funt processiun la dedenz en cel encloistre;
La femme lu rei Hugun, ke sa corune en portet,
Par la main tent sa fille, ke ad la crine bloie.
Hu que veit Oliver, volenters i parolt;
825   Fait lui contenance gente, amisté li portet,
Volenters le baisast, mais pur sun pere nen oset.
Il entrent al muster cum il issent de l'encloistre.
Li ercevasque Turpin, ki maistre fud des ordres,
Il lur cantat la messe, e li barnét i ofret.
830   Puis venent al palais, si demeinent grant baldorie.

LIII

Franceis sunt al palais, tuz fud prest li digners.
Les tabeles furent drecees e sunt alez manger.
Nule ren que il demandent ne lur fud demuréd;
Asez unt veneisun de cerf e de sengler,
835   E unt grues e gantes e pouns enpeverez,
A espandant lur portent le vin e le clarét,

---

807 mei   808 cel clos   811 graidre   815 nortre   820 la nostre
821 ferunt   822 le crin   830 demeinant   836 Espandant

LI

'My lord', said Charlemagne to King Hugo the Strong,
'Now you are my vassal, with all your men as witnesses.
Today we must celebrate and enjoy ourselves lavishly
805   And wear our golden crowns together;
As a mark of friendship, I am prepared to wear mine.'
'And I, my lord, mine, with your agreement;
We shall walk together in procession within this cloister.'
Charlemagne wears his great crown of gold,
810   King Hugo wears his, just a little lower;
Charlemagne was taller by a good foot and three inches.
The Franks look at them, they spoke with one voice:
'My lady the queen spoke foolishly and wrongly.
Charles is a man of great worth when it comes to a display of strength;
815   We shall never enter any land without the honour being ours.'

LII

Charlemagne wears his crown in Constantinople,
King Hugo wears his still lower.
The Franks look at them, many utter these words:
'My lady the queen spoke very foolishly
820   When she valued other barons as highly as ourselves.'
Thus they walk together in procession in the cloister.
King Hugo's wife, who wears her crown,
Holds the hand of her fair-haired daughter.
As soon as she sees Oliver, she wishes to speak to him.
825   She puts on a fair expression and shows her affection for him.
She would like to have kissed him, but dares not because of her father.
They enter the church when they come out of the cloister.
Archbishop Turpin, the highest-ranking priest,
Sang Mass to them and the barons make their offering.
830   Then they come to the palace where there is great rejoicing.

LIII

The Franks are in the palace, the dinner was ready;
The tables were set up and they went to eat.
Nothing which they desire was slow in coming;
They have venison and boar's meat in plenty,
835   And cranes, geese and peppered peacocks.
The wine and the claret are served in abundance,

E cantent e vielent e rotent cil geugler.
Li reis Hugue li Forz ad Carlemaine apeléd:
'Trestuz mes granz tresor vus seit abandunez!
840   Tant en prengent Franceis cum il en volderunt porter.'
E dist li emperere: 'Tut iço lassét ester!
Ja ne prendrai del vostre un dener muneéd;
Ja unt il tant del mon que il nel poent porter.
Mes cungét nus dunét: nus en cuvent aler.'
845   E dist Hugue li Forz: 'Jo nel vus os veer!'
Les mulz lur tint l'em as marbrins degreez.
E dist l'emperere: 'Sicum vus cumandez!'
Wunt sei entrebaiser, a Deu sunt cumandez.

LIV

Quant Franceis unt mangét, des ore s'en irrunt.
850   Les mulz e les sumers lur tint om as peruns,
Si sunt muntez Franceis que a joie s'en vunt.
La fille lu rei Hugun i curt tut a bandun;
La u veit Oliver, sil prent par sun gerun:
'A vus ai jo turnét ma amistét e ma amur;
855   Que m'en porterez en France, si m'en irrai od vus!'
'Bele', dist Oliver, 'm'amur vus abandun;
Jo m'en irrai en France od mun seignur Carleun.'

LV

Mult fu liéd e joius Carlemaine li ber,
Ki tel rei ad cunquis sanz bataille campel.
860   Que vus en ai jo mes lunc plait a cunter?
Il passent les pais, les estrange regnez,
Venuz sunt a Paris, a la bone citét,
E vunt a Saint Denis, al muster sunt entrez;
Karlemaine se culcget a oreisuns, li ber.
865   Quant il ad Deu preiét, si s'en est relevét;
Le clou e la corune si ad mis sur l'auter,
E les altres reliques depart par sun regnét.
Iloec fud la reine, al pied li est caiét;
Sun mautalent li ad li reis tut perdunét,
870   Pur l'amur del sepulcre que il ad aurét.

---

839 seint   840 parter   842 Ia nen p.   844 Mes des ore le cunget
nus en dunet cuvent aler   847 leperere

And the jongleurs sing and play on their vielles and their rotes.
King Hugo the Strong has called to Charlemagne:
'Let all my great treasure be placed at your disposal!
840 Let the Franks take away as much as they can carry.'
The emperor said: 'Let's hear no more of this!
I shall not take a single minted penny of yours;
They already have more from me than they can carry.
But give us leave, we have to go.'
845 And King Hugo the Strong said: 'I dare not refuse you'.
The mules were held for them at the marble steps.
The emperor said: 'As you wish'.
They embrace each other and commend each other to God.

LIV

When the Franks have eaten, they soon set off.
850 The mules and the packhorses were held for them at the blocks;
The Franks mounted and set off filled with joy.
King Hugo's daughter comes rushing forward;
When she sees Oliver, she seizes him by the side of his cloak:
'I have given you my love and my affection;
855 Take me off to France and I shall come with you.'
'Fair one', said Oliver, 'my love is yours completely;
But I will go off to France with my lord Charlemagne.'

LV

Charlemagne the Brave was filled with joy and happiness
That he had overcome such a king without a pitched battle.
860 Why more can I say to prolong my story?
They pass through the countries and the foreign lands,
And they arrived in Paris, the good city;
And they go to Saint-Denis, they have entered the church.
Charlemagne the Brave prostrates himself in prayer.
865 When he has prayed to God, he rose to his feet again;
The nail and the crown he has placed on the altar,
And the other relics he distributes throughout his kingdom.
The queen was there, she has fallen at his feet.
The king abandoned his resentment against her,
870 For love of the sepulchre at which he has worshipped.

NOTES TO THE TEXT AND TRANSLATION

Unless otherwise stated, references in these notes to Aebischer are to his second edition of the text, those to Koschwitz are to his later editions and those to Horrent to his *Le Pèlerinage de Charlemagne: essai d'explication littéraire.*

1. The text begins and ends in the great and ancient abbey (now basilica) of Saint Denis, a little to the north of Paris, which was closely associated with the kings of France, most of whom were buried there. In 775 A.D. Charlemagne himself consecrated the third church on the site. In the twelfth century it was of central importance in the religious, artistic and political life of France. From 1140, under Abbot Suger, the church was splendidly rebuilt in the new Gothic style. Queens were traditionally crowned there. It may well be that the crowds participating in the Lendit, the great fair and holiday which celebrated its relics of the Passion, were the first audience for the *Pèlerinage* (see Bédier, IV, pp. 137-56, Coulet, pp. 211-13). See G. M. Spiegel, *The Chronicle Tradition of Saint-Denis: A Survey* (Brookline NY and Leyden: Classical Folia, 1978), pp. 11-37.

3. *Sa espee* is a typically Anglo-Norman spelling of *s'espee*; cf. *me espee* (v. 25), and also *de ascer* (= *d'ascer*, v. 172), *le aguilun* (v. 286), etc.

14. *Sa* is a reduced Anglo-Norman spelling of *sai.*

39. *Frez* is a reduced Anglo-Norman form of *ferez*; cf. also *frai* (v. 42, etc.), *frunt* (v. 186, etc.). On the other hand, Anglo-Norman scribes frequently add *e* between *dr* (*aspanderai*, v. 776), *tr* (*abaterai*, v. 514) and *vr* (*averai*, v. 57). In this poem this *e* does not have syllabic value.

43. MS *estorcer*, emended by Koschwitz, Aebischer, Picherit and de Riquer to *estordre*, is more likely to represent an original *estortre.*

56. Editors emend *ne* to *nel* here, but the addition of an object or complement for the verb *penser* does not necessarily make the line easier to translate. Cooper gives 'Jamais vous ne devriez penser à ma puissance', Tyssens 'Vous n'auriez pas dû penser cela de ma puissance' and Picherit 'You should not have thought so poorly of my power'.

63. MS *Berin* is normally emended to *Gerin.* The same personage appears again in v. 602 under the form *Genin.* The reference appears to be to Gerin, companion of Gerer in the

Chanson de Roland (vv. 107, 174, etc.).

81. In view of the fact that the Franks depart on mules (v. 89) and as pilgrims (vv. 79-80, 86-88), some editors have been disturbed by the presence here of war-horses. Koschwitz considers this line to be an interpolation. Favati, Picherit and de Riquer want the line to read 'They do not have war-horses shod in front and behind' (Picherit) and they emend *E funt ferrer* to *N'i funt ferrer*. However, these war-horses are mentioned again in v. 340 (Picherit emends *destrers* in this line to *somiers* 'pack-horses'). See Horrent, p. 27 (n.3), Aebischer, p. 87, and Tyssens, p. 35.

100-08. The journey of Charles and his men from France to Jerusalem has puzzled readers of this text, some of whom have questioned the order of the lines in the manuscript. Koschwitz places vv. 102-03 after vv. 105-06, letting v. 104 follow v. 101. MS *la liee* in v. 103 is normally emended to *Lalice* and interpreted as one of the cities bearing the name Laodicea. Aebischer in his first edition emends to *Lalie* and in his second edition to *Lalice* (see his note on p. 88). The form *Lalice* has, however, been interpreted as referring to the province of Lycia in southern Turkey. The reading *croiz ptie* (=*partie* or *pertie*) is emended by Koschwitz to *Croatie*. Aebischer, Favati and Picherit maintain *Croiz Partie*, as does the present edition. Tyssens translates as 'La région de la Croix'. Nicholls emends *Croiz* to *Troie* and interprets as 'the region of Troy'. This is a tempting emendation, but it has the disadvantage of making a twelve-syllable line hypermetric. The area referred to as *Romanie* in v. 106 could be either the Byzantine Empire as a whole or just the Adriatic part. It is not clear exactly where the Franks are evisaged as meeting Turks, Persians and the 'gent haie' (v. 102). The 'hated people' are presumably Saracens or Arabs. Horrent's interpretation ('la gent haïssable des Turcs et des Persans') assumes that the phrase is in apposition to 'les Turcs et les Persaunz'. The *flum* in v. 103 is presumably whichever waterway the author or the compiler of a map would see as dividing Europe from Asia, perhaps here the Dardanelles. Another interpretation of the passage is provided by Pinson, who sees Charles as taking the route followed by Peter the Hermit. *Croix Partie* would be Croatia and the *flum* the River Sara in Yugoslavia. Pinson suggests that the espression *a la liee* could refer to the way the planks in the boats crossing the river were joined together (*liee*=*ligata*). More recently, Bennett ('*La grant ewe del flum*', p. 482, n.30) identifies the *flum* as the Danube and *la liee* as the River Aliuta (now Olt) on the border of Bulgaria and the Byzantine Empire.

113. Picherit interprets 'un muster de marbre peint a volte' as 'a marble church with painted vaults' and Tyssens as 'une église voûtée de marbre polychrome'. The author is particularly keen to indicate the presence of vaulted ceilings in the buildings he describes (see vv. 347, 422, 663) and paintings (see vv. 124, 345, 422).

114. In his use of the Church of St Paternoster the poet combines elements of three ancient churches in Jerusalem. He uses the name of the Church of the Paternoster on the Mount of Olives (on the site of a modern church of the same name). He locates it on the site of the Last Supper, traditionally attributed to the place on Mount Sion occupied now by the Church of the Dormition, formerly by the Church of St Mary of Mount Sion (also known as the Church of the Apostles). He gives his church the splendid decoration of the Church of the Holy Sepulchre.

125. Aebischer translates *de grant majestez* as 'peintures magnifiques' and Tyssens as 'de grandes figures en majesté'. The term *majestez* seems to refer to an image of God or the Virgin Mary seated in majesty.

127. The term *lavacre* (Latin *lavacrum*) refers either to baptismal water (Picherit, Tyssens) or simply to any running water (Aebischer, de Riquer). Koschwitz omits *lavacre* entirely.

134. In the Eastern Church the title of patriarch was bestowed on bishops of the five principal sees of Constantinople, Antioch, Alexandria, Jerusalem and Rome.

142. MS *ses clers en albe la citet* has been variously emended and interpreted. Koschwitz reads *ses clers en albes atirez* and Aebischer *ses clers en albe atiret*. In the present edition *en* has been added with Favati and Picherit before *la citet*. Cooper interprets *albe* as 'dawn', but it undoubtedly refers to the long white linen vestment worn by priests. In fact, the expression *clers en albe* might well mean little more than 'priests'.

157. The form *mames* (Old French *meïsmes*), normally emended to *maimes* or *meimes*, occurs again in v. 769. See also the form *aparmames* in v. 163. The form *maimes* is found in v. 560.

158. Since Koschwitz, editors have agreed that the patriarch intends to bestow on Charles the name Charles Maines / Charlemaines. This would be the first use of this name, and any earlier use by way of editorial intervention would therefore not be valid. Readers of Aebischer's edition, for example, have already encountered the full name several times (vv. 1, 17, 112, 123, etc.). In the manuscript, the forms *Karlemaines* and *Carlemaines*

(sometimes abbreviated) occur only after v. 158. For the structural importance of the concept of 'greatness' see Sturm, pp. 14-15.

173. *Predicét* is the past participle of *predicher*, a learned variant of Old French *prëechier* (Modern French *prêcher*) 'to preach'.

185. The last two letters of the manuscript reading *cundistid* are expunged. Editors are divided concerning whether to take *a* as the auxiliary verb of a perfect tense (Koschwitz in his early editions, Picherit) or as a prefix of the verb *acunduire* (Koschwitz, later editions, Aebischer, de Riquer). In the context a perfect tense seems appropriate.

198. The term *fert(e)re* can be masculine or feminine, so there is no need to emend *une* to *un* with Koschwitz, Picherit and other editors. Aebischer omits *une* and reads *faire fertre*.

201. The term *menuz* has been interpreted in different ways. Cooper thinks that the reliquary is bound with 'de nombreuses bandes d'argent', whereas Aebischer and de Riquer see it as bound carefully ('avec soin', 'cuidadosamente'). Picherit thinks that it is bound 'closely' and Tyssens that the bands of silver are very close together ('très rapprochées'). As *menuz* often seems to convey the notion of a repeated action, Cooper's interpretation has been adopted here (but perhaps there are 'several' rather than 'many' bands).

208-09. The allusion here is to the Church of St Mary Latin. The form in the manuscript is *Latanie* and it is tempting to emend with other editors to *Latinie*. Although the author does not allude to the fact, the Church of St Mary Latin, near the Holy Sepulchre (and set, as in the poem, among markets) was so called because of its connections with the Western, Latin-speaking Church. It was reputed to have been founded by Charlemagne. It was certainly, even before the Crusades, the church of a Western, Benedictine abbey (see Paris, pp. 22-25, and Heinermann, pp. 533-34). Spitzer interpreted *language* as a term designating 'les groupes nationaux étrangers' (p. 21) and Levy saw it as a generic term indicating 'any community of people having a language of its own' (1947, p. 127). See also Favati, p. 159, Richard and Tyssens, p. 41.

210-12. Both *pailes* and *series* (Old French *siries*) seem to refer to silk fabrics. *Series* (Latin *sericum* 'silk') is rendered by Picherit as 'damask' (a silk fabric from the city of Damascus). The Modern French equivalent, borrowed by English, is 'serge', a twilled cotton, silk, or rayon fabric. *Pailes* (Latin *pallium*) is a frequently used term in this text and in the French epic in general. *Coste* is either costmary (*costum Maria*, also called alecost) or ginger

(Koschwitz, Aebischer). Costmary is a herbaceous plant (*Chrysanthemum balsamita*) with fragrant leaves, native to Asia, but now grown in southern Europe and used as a seasoning. *Canele* is cinnamon.

213. Probably a reminiscence of Jesus's remarks concerning the traders and money-changers in the temple of Jerusalem (Matthew 21. 12-13, Mark 11 .15-17, etc.), here directed at the merchants of modern Jerusalem. The visit of Jesus to the temple is linked in Matthew (21. 14) to the healing of the blind and the lame (see vv. 192-95 and 257-58 in the present text).

216. The form *donét* is one of several Anglo-Norman second person plural forms with *t* encountered in this text (in the imperative, present indicative and future). See *gardét* (vv. 224, 509), *conusét* (v. 305), *atendét* (v. 397), *verrét* (v. 523), *comandét* (v. 580), *gaberét* (v. 661) and *hunisét* (v. 721).

226-32. There has been discussion concerning a possible lacuna after v. 228 and whether or not to open a new *laisse* at v. 229. Lines 226-28 have an assonance in *i* and vv. 229-32 in *ei*. Koschwitz in his first edition corrected the forms in *i* to *ei*. In his more recent editions, he indicates a lacuna at the end of v. 229, emends *aveir* and *remaner* in v. 229 and v. 230 to *aveir* and *remaneir*, and has a *laisse* XlVb beginning at v. 226. Favati corrects the forms in *e* and *ei* to *i*.

260-61. The journey from Jerusalem to Constantinople is vague. Editors are divided over the interpretation of *monteles* as either 'mountains' (Koschwitz, who emends to *montaignes*, Favati, Picherit) or a place named Muntelés (Aebischer, 'nom imaginaire d'une région de l'Asie Mineure', p. 113). The *Puis d'Abilant* have been seen as 'the Anti-Lebanon mountain range between Lebanon and Syria' (Picherit, p. 78, see Horrent, p. 50, n.2), but Aebischer regards Abilant as another 'nom imaginaire' (p. 95). The *Roche del Guitume* has been identified as the statue of Lot in salt near the Dead Sea, which is geographically unlikely, as Charles would be travelling north at this time. Aebischer again thinks this an imaginary location (p. 113). See Favati, p. 163, and Tyssens, p. 44.

263. *Cloches* is interpreted by Aebischer and de Riquer as 'bells', but printed by Favati and Picherit as *clochés* 'bell-towers'. Koschwitz emends to *clochiers*. Aebischer felt strongly that the correct form was *cloches* (pp. 88-89). The term *egles* refers to metal ornaments in the shape of eagles on roofs and towers rather than to 'churches' (Koschwitz, Favati). See Tyssens, p. 44.

266. Koschwitz replaces *glazaus* (which, together with *beaus* in v. 265, is a false assonance) with *aiglenz* 'eglantine, sweetbrier'. Aebischer and Picherit adopt this suggestion, but Favati and de Riquer retain *glazaus* (Latin *gladiolus*).

281. The substantive *paile* is normally masculine, but it can be feminine. Some editors emend *cele* to *cel* to establish a correct syllable count.

288. Aebischer, Favati and de Riquer preserve the reading of the manuscript: *Une caiere sus le tent d'or suzpendant*. Koschwitz emends to *Une chaiere sus tienent d'or sozpendant* and Picherit to *Une caiere d'or le sustent en pendant*. See Picherit, 'Sur le vers 288 du *Voyage de Charlemagne à Jérusalem et à Constantinople*', *Zeitschrift für romanische Philologie*, 99 (1983), 512-13. The meaning seems fairly clear, but no arrangement of the words is entirely satisfactory.

294. Tyssens, de Riquer and Picherit interpret *grizain* as Greek. Cf. Tobler-Lommatzsch, IV, 675, *grisan* 'grauer Mantelstoff'.

296. Favati and Picherit maintain the unattested *arét*, but Koschwitz prints *arere* and Aebischer *arei*. See Favati, pp. 167-69, and Tyssens, p. 46. Editors normally suppress *a* in this line and take *condut* as a present tense. An alternative reading would be *acondut* (the verb *aconduire* occurs in v. 752, see also v. 705).

310. The form *Hugun* occurs in the manuscript both as subject (vv. 310, 323, 394, etc.) and as object (vv. 46, 283, 302). It also occurs in the forms *Hugu* (vv. 303, 478, 483) and *Hug'* (as subject, vv. 567, 584, 590, 620, etc., and as object, vv. 670, 682, 778, 785, etc.).

318. The normal sense of *amunt* is 'higher up', but the line here reads awkwardly and Tyssens suggests the meaning 'largement' (translation, p. 11) or 'en quantité' (commentary, p. 48).

328. The form *peals* has been related to either *piz* 'pikes' or *peuz* 'stakes'. For *escansue* Koschwitz, Aebischer and Picherit have *aconseüe*, from *aconsivre*. De Riquer keeps *escansue* and translates by the verb 'desarmar' ('to dismantle, take to pieces'). Favati, adopting a suggestion of Horrent that the substantive *escansue* 'accident' is relevant here (p. 54, n. 4), reads *a l'escansue*.

340. See note to v. 81.

347. The form *vout* clearly means 'vaulted'. It has been variously emended to *volut*, *voltiz*, *votuz* and *voutuz*. *Cloanz*, present participle of *clore* 'close', is translated by Aebischer as

'couvert', by Cooper as 'dessus fermé' and by Picherit as 'topped with a tight dome'.

348. It is not clear whether the expression *par compas* refers to the circular shape of the palace or to the skill with which it was constructed. In v. 428 the expression *a cumpas* refers to the construction of the thirteenth bed, reserved for Charlemagne.

350-61. The description of King Hugo's palace almost certainly contains echoes of contemporary Constantinople, as Gaston Paris thought. The statues which announce the coming of the storm are a reflection of a real pair over the Boukoleon Gate. The gate, which was one of the main access points from the east, owed its name to the notion of horns sounding in the wind. The great palace of Constantinople contained a splendid banqueting hall, the Chrysotriclinos, which had a vaulted circular roof with sixteen windows, silver doors and abundant mosaic decorations representing a garden full of flowers. At the side of this room was the Triclinos with nineteen beds. The emperor used to invite twelve guests to recline there at his circular table during the twelve feast days from Christmas to Epiphany. Of particular interest to our poem is the motif of the rotating palace. It is possible that this reflects a form of optical illusion connected with hemispherical domes. 'Apparently if one gazed long enough at a circular church dome with its many lights, the whole thing seemed to move' (Schlauch, 'The Palace of Hugon de Constantinople', p. 503). It would also have been conceivable, as Polak suggests (p. 164), to have set the floor in motion by the use of some apparatus below, like a winch. But the text compares the movement of the palace to the shaft of a windmill ('Altresi le fait turner cum arbre de mulin', v. 371). A horizontal Persian windmill, activated by strong winds from a constant direction, could have been built to power automata (Polak, pp. 164-65). For parallels between the description of the palace and Greek romances, Irish literature and classical texts, such as Ovid's *Metamorphoses*, see Schlauch, and Walton, 'The Palace of Hugon'.

366-67. The names Alixandre and Constantin are easily recognisable as Alexander the Great (356-323 B.C., King of Macedon and conqueror of Greece, Egypt and the Persian Empire), and Constantine, first Christian Roman Emperor, who became sole emperor of East and West in 325 A.D. and moved his capital to Byzantium, renaming it Constantinople, in 330 A.D. *Crisanz* is more difficult to identify. Originally thought to be Trajan or Caesar, he is now normally seen as Crescentius, who held Hadrian's Mausoleum in Rome against Otto III at the end of the tenth century (see Paris, pp. 45-46). The attribution to him of a large number of buildings ('tanz honurs') owes far more to legend than to history.

381. The form *braines* in the manuscript is probably to be read as *brames* or *brasmes* 'quartz'. Translators take *utremarin* to mean 'beyond the sea'. It could perhaps be taken as a colour term (Medieval Latin *ultramarinus*), indicating a deep purplish-blue colour, or, more specifically, as referring to the pigment of sodium and aluminum silicates obtained by powdering mineral lapis lazuli.

384. The term *costis*, unattested elsewhere, has given rise to numerous conjectures. Levy emended to *tostis* 'quick, violent', but since Horrent it has been interpreted as relating to the notion of 'side' or 'coast' (Old French *costé*, *costel*). Tyssens translates as 'de biais' and Picherit as 'as it blew in from the coast'(Aebischer, 'violent et latéral', combines two possible meanings). But it seems unlikely that *costis* is connected with the notion of 'side', as its meaning must be similar to that of *gres* and *hidus*. It is probably an adjective capable of being accompanied by the adverb *mult*, which would not be possible for the meaning 'from the side, from the coast'. Godefroy (II, 325b) and Tobler-Lommatzsch (II, p. 941) link the term to the verb *coster* 'cost, trouble'. The adjective *costus* is attested with the meanings 'troublesome, harmful, irksome', as well as 'costly'.

406. The reference to Dun has provoked a good deal of discussion. Michel identified the town as Châteaudun (Eure-et-Loir) and this was supported by Paris, who pointed out that only three other towns in France are mentioned in the text: Paris, Saint-Denis and Chartres. Koschwitz in his first edition emended to *Dijon*, but he later accepted the identification as Verdun. Favati reads *adun* 'together', followed by a suggested lacuna. See Tyssens, p. 53, who translates as 'en la ville de Dun'.

412. The term *clarez* has been translated into French as 'claret' (Cooper), 'clairet' (Tyssens), and 'hydromel' (Aebischer) and into English as 'clary' (Picherit). It is not certain how *claret* would have been made in the twelfth century, but it is not the equivalent of Modern French *clairet* or English *claret*. In France at the time of the *Pèlerinage* it would have been a piment, made from a blend of white and red wine (from Burgundy or Bordeaux) with honey, spices and other aromatics added. It could have been light red or yellowish in colour. Hippocras was very similar to 'clarry', but it was made of either white or red wine, not a blend. See H. W. Allen, *A History of Wine* (London: Faber and Faber, 1961, pp. 161-68). Note that the wine in our text is actually drunk in Constantinople. For want of a more

satisfactory equivalent, the term 'claret' has been adopted in the present translation.

413. The *vielle* was a fiddle, oval in shape, with at least three strings. The *rote* was a five-stringed harp, rather like a zither. Line 413 is repeated at v. 837. By indicating the presence of imaginary colleagues on such a respectable occasion, the poet here is taking the opportunity to advertise the social utility of performers such as himself.

424. The *rei Golias* is almost certainly Goliath of Gath, the Biblical Philistine slain by David (I Samuel 18).

430-31. Maseuz is clearly represented as a fairy, so she cannot be seen as Maheut or Matilda, wife of William the Conqueror, who, with her ladies, the legend has it, embroidered the Bayeux Tapestry (see Tyssens, p. 54). MS *q li reis dunat* is variously emended (Koschwitz and Picherit *qui le rei le dunat*, Aebischer *qui li reis le dunat*, Favati and de Riquer *que li reis le dunat*). The normal translation is 'who gave it to the king', but *li reis* could conceivably be interpreted as the subject: 'to whom the king gave, whom the king rewarded for her efforts'.

433-34. Cooper translates these lines as 'Ils devaient bien aimer le roi qui les quittait, / Qui les avait si bien servis et pourvus'. In this interpretation it would seem that the king in v. 433 is Charles, not Hugo, and the remark would constitute an intervention by the poet, who would thereby be stressing the lack of gratitude on the part of the Franks when they indulge in their *gabs*.

446. From its first occurrence in this line, the verb *gab(b)er* (and the related substantives *gab* and *gabement*) plays a dominant role in the poem. The verb occurs twenty-one times, the substantive *gabement* three times and the forms *gab*, *gabs* or *gas* thirteen times. The act of *gaber* is both to jest and to mock. In the mouth of the Franks, it is an intransitive verb, 'to jest', i.e. to outline, verbally and with comic intent, a superhuman feat related to one's surroundings. But, as used by others (the spy, King Hugo and the angel), it is a transitive verb, 'to mock, to make insulting or provocative remarks about' (vv. 626, 630, 643, 676). In this text the notion of the *gab* is linked to several other themes: foolishness, exaggeration, the misinterpretation of something heard or seen, and the teaching of a lesson (v. 661). See Introduction, pp. xxx-xxxix, and Cobby, *Ambivalent Conventions*, pp. 101-07, 143-45.

488. It looks at first sight as if the poet is using an expression *aveir testimonie de* 'to have one's way with', and Koschwitz in his first two editions has 'Se jo n'ai testimonie de li anut

cent feiz'. Aebischer has 'Si jo n'ai testimonie anut de li cent feiz', but he claims (1962, pp. 830-31) that he has been unable to find an example of this usage. It is more likely that the expression *testimonie de lui* means 'by her testimony', and editors, including Koschwitz in his later editions ('tesmoign de li'), place a comma before and after this expression (the position in the line of *anut* varies from editor to editor). The verb *aveir* would thus be used in the sense of 'to take, to possess' a woman. King Hugo himself uses the verb in this sense in v. 694.

514. The *teise* is a unit of measure of just under two metres (see v. 750).

581-82. The almandine is a deep red or violet garnet. It owes its name to the ancient city of Alabanda in Asia Minor, where these gemstones were first cut. In v. 582 Koschwitz, Aebischer and Picherit emend *mage* to *marage* (Favati and de Riquer have *image*). The form *sur* in the manuscript is expunged. Koschwitz, Aebischer and Picherit emend to *fait ultre mer*. Favati indicates a lacuna (*que fud faiz [...] en mer*). De Riquer maintains both *sur* and *en*. The idea of Aimer's hat being made overseas ('Made overseas with the skin of a big fish', Picherit) or at sea ('Confectionné en mer avec la peau d'un grand poisson marin', Tyssens) is unsatisfactory. One wonders whether at one stage there was a band or an object of pure gold on his hat and thus whether the text once contained the expression *d'or mer* 'of pure gold' (see vv. 3, 543), which later became *sor mer* by confusion with *marage*. Commentators have been puzzled by Aimer's boast. It is normally assumed that he plans to become invisible 'thanks to the stones or to the fish skin of his hat' (Picherit, p. 81). See Koschwitz, pp. 82-84, and Horrent, pp. 72-73.

594. Koschwitz, followed by Cavaliere and supported by Tyssens, emends *pin* to *pui*. This seems unnecessary and thematically undesirable. See note to v. 780. Tyssens suggests that *antif* should be read as *autif* 'high'. She translates as 'au sommet de ce mont altier'.

624. The manuscript reading *Ois les parler* is often emended to *Oistes les parler*. In his first edition Aebischer has *Oï les as parler* and in his second *Oïstes les parler*. The manuscript form *remaindrum* is often emended to *remaindrunt* (*remandront*, Koschwitz). The king is seen as asking whether the Franks will remain faithful to him or whether they will stay with him. But Aebischer prints *si remaindrum ami* 'if we shall remain friends'.

658. Koschwitz and Picherit replace *volenters* with *certes*. Favati and de Riquer maintain *par vionage*, but Koschwitz, Aebischer and Picherit emend to *par guionage*.

Aebischer glosses *guionage* as 'gage, remise en nantissement', and Tyssens translates the line as 'Et je vous en rendrai volontiers raison avec caution'. Picherit translates as 'Then I shall gladly hold myself responsible for them, on my word'. Cf. also Bennett, '"Si vus en respondrai volenters par guionage"'.

659-61. Koschwitz and Picherit indicate a lacuna at the end of v. 659. If this is correct, the gap would be filled by a reply from Charlemagne.

672. It is clear that this line indicates that God sent down an angel to speak with the Franks. But can the verb *aparceveir* be interpreted with Koschwitz as a transitive verb ('erscheinen lassen, senden')? This would mean that the *qui* in the manuscript has to be interpreted as an oblique form (Picherit emends to *que*, Koschwitz and Aebischer to *cui*). Favati retains *qui* as a subject case and prints the phrase as 'qui, Deus! i aparut'.

701. Charlemagne evidently wishes to say that it would be wrong for Hugo to let Oliver off, to exempt him from fulfilling his boast. But it seems that a word is missing at the end of the line. Editors tend to add *quite*, but Aebischer prefers *vivre* and he also emends *len* to *les*.

719. Editors print this line in different ways. Koschwitz indicates a lacuna of one line between *ço* and *ne*. Favati removes *ço* and Aebischer has 'Mes volentez cumplir, ço jo ne quier par veir!'. De Riquer and Picherit, who translates as 'I truly wish that you allow me to carry it out', remove the negative particle. Tyssens renders the line as 'C'est avec votre accord que je veux l'accomplir'. See Picherit, p. 81, and Aebischer, 'Sur Quelques Passages', pp. 833-85.

723. The form *cuvent* must be interpreted with Favati as the third person singular, present tense of *cuvenir*. Koschwitz emends to the substantive *covenant*. Aebischer, Picherit and de Riquer emend to *de men cuvent*. See Tyssens, p. 72.

726. Koschwitz, Picherit and de Riquer change the order of the manuscript, placing *mes* before *la nuit*. Favati retains the manuscript order, but suppresses *que*. Aebischer refused to include the line. Deeply concerned for Oliver's reputation, he has written extensively on the question. In 1956 he allowed Oliver to fulfil his pledge by kissing the girl one hundred times: *Li quens ne li baisat la nuit mes que cent feiz*. In 1962, in reaction to the discussion by Horrent (pp. 98-100), he went on to claim that 'Le vers 726 était cancellé dans le manuscrit du British Museum' (p. 839). Certainly, two scholars, Koch and Wülcker, who examined the manuscript before its disappearance in 1879, informed Koschwitz that the line

was cancelled using lighter ink than that used for the scribe's own corrections, and he tells us that the line was struck through (p. 40, see also his note to vv. 237 and 735, and Aebischer, 1962, p. 839). See also Brians, Deroy, Favati, p. 205, and Tyssens, pp. 73-74. On the importance of courtliness in this scene (the term *curteis* appears in vv. 710, 716 and 725), see Introduction, p. xxxvi, and my article, 'The Term *courtois* in Twelfth-Century French'.

746. The form *neiles*, unattested elsewhere, has troubled editors. Picherit translates the line as 'By their silk aglets he hurls them to the ground'. This interpretation is based on a suggestion by J. Wathelet-Willem, reported by Horrent (p. 101, n. 1), that *neiles* is equivalent to *nasle*, attested under the form *naliere* 'aglet'. Any translation must take into account the violent action implied by the expression *jeter jus*. Tyssens sees William as hurling his beaver furs into the silk hangings draping the walls: 'Et les jette dans les tentures de soie.' For this purpose *neiles* is read as *veiles* 'curtains, hangings' (see M. Tyssens, 'Encore les "neisles de paile" (*Karlsreise*, v. 746)', *Marche Romane*, 26, 1976, 19-30).

753. Some editors (e.g. Favati, Picherit) emend *fenduz* to *fend* and incorporate this line in the following laisse.

780. Here, as in vv. 594, 760 and 783, Koschwitz emends *pin* to *pui* (see note to v. 594). But the notion of Charlemagne and his companions being huddled together in a pine tree to escape the flood waters, incongruous as it may seem, is an effective comic image. The poet may have had in mind several links, between the pine tree in which the Franks take refuge and Hugo's threat to hang them from a pine tree (v. 760), between this comic scene of Charlemagne's embarrassment and the initial scene beneath an olive tree which sets the whole story going (v. 7), and with the council scene in the *Chanson de Roland*, which takes place 'desuz un pin"' (v. 168). But Aebischer's suggestion (p. 94) that in our text *desur* 'in' should be emended to *desuz* 'beneath' surely robs the scene of its comic impact. See Cobby, *Ambivalent Conventions*, pp. 162-63.

820. Aebischer, Picherit and Tyssens present the manuscript reading as *preisat*, but it can also be interpreted as *purisat* (Favati). Editors either insert a word after *que* or after *preisat* (*que ja preisat barnet*, Koschwitz; *que preisat sun barnet*, Aebischer; *qu'ele preisat barnet*, Picherit; *que preisat tel barnet*, de Riquer). Picherit translates the line as 'When she judged that any worthiness could match ours', and Tyssens as 'En estimant qu'une noblesse pût

égaler la nôtre'. Favati thinks that a verb with a negative force is required and emends to *mespreisat*.

825. On the expression *faire contenant / contenance gent(e)* see my article 'Old French *contenance* and *contenant*', esp. pp. 24-26. In this edition, the MS *contenance* has been retained.

869. On *perduner* in the sense of 'abandon, lay aside' see my article '*Talent* in Early Old French (to 1150)', *Romania*, 95 (1974), 443-66, pp. 456-57.

INDEX OF PROPER NAMES

Forms given are those found in the French text. The expression 'see note' refers to the relevant line of the section 'Notes to the Text and Translation'

Abilant 260, perhaps the Anti-Lebanon mountain range between Lebanon and Syria, or just an imaginary location

Aimer 579, **Haimer** 64, one of the twelve peers

Aimeri 765, **Ameri** 739, father of William of Orange

Alixandre 366, Alexander the Great

Amiral, l' 432, the Emir

Antioche 49, Antioch

Arabie 199, Arabia

Baivere 101, Bavaria

Berenger 63, 540, one of the twelve peers

Berin 63, one of the twelve peers. Also called **Genin** 602. Presumably the same as Gerin in the *Chanson de Roland*

Bernard (de Brusban) 65, 553, 764, 771, son of Aimeri de Narbonne and one of the twelve peers

Bertram 65, 94, 565, 591, **Berteram** 327, son of Bernard de Brusban, nephew of William and one of the twelve peers

Brusban, see **Bernard**

Burgoine 100, Burgundy

Capadoce 48, Cappadocia (Asia Minor)

Carle 365, 320, 400, **Carles**, 91, 112, 393, 603, 629, **Carleun** 303, 857, **Carlun** 298, 333, 494, **Charle** 17, 39, 41, 51, **Charles**, 30, 342, **Charles Maines** 158, Charlemagne

Carlemaigne, 791, **Carlemain**, 419, 504, **Carlemaine**, 396, 445, 451, 652, 662, 673, 674, 679, 683, 700, 732, 736, 752, 772, 795, 799, 802, 838, 858, **Carlemaines** 300, 307, 453, 485, 762, 783, Charlemagne

Cartres 654, Chartres

Charle(s), see **Carles**

Cristus, 676, Christ

Costantin 366, the Emperor Constantine

Costuntinoble 47, **Constantinoble** 262, **Costentinoble** 816, Constantinople

Crisans de Rome 367, Crescentius (see note)

Croiz Partie, 104 (see note)

Dam(p)nedeu, 69, 91, 252, 772, 782, the Lord God

Deu(s), 32, 68, 107, 115, etc., God, Christ

Denemarche 519, Denmark

Dun 406. Identification uncertain (see note)

Ernalz (de Girunde) 64, 566, son of Aimeri de Narbonne and one of the twelve peers

Espaine 230, Spain

Estefne 165, St Stephen

France 58, 66, 76, 86, 100, 151, 161, 214, 233, 327, 406, 654, 679, 711, 786, 855, 857

Franceis 23, 88, 223, 237, 315, 393, 399, 414, 445, 623, 649, 655, 681, 812, 818, 831, 840, 849, 851, the Franks

Genin 602, see **Berin**

Girunde, see **Ernalz**

Golias 424, Goliath

Grece 47, 105, Greece

Guillames 744, see **Willeme (de Orenge)**

Guitume (Roche del), 261, the Rock of Guitume. Perhaps the statue of Lot in salt near the Dead Sea, or just an imaginary location (see note)

Haimer, see **Aimer**

Hugue, 567, 584, 590, 563, 601, 620, 628, 642, 810, 817, 838, 845, **Hugun**, 46, 283, 302, 303, 310, 323, 394, 397, 401, 419, 437, 444, 454, 466, 471, 478, 483, 533, 559, 660, 670, 682, 692, 753, 764, 778, 785, 800, 803, 807, 822, 852, Hugo, King of Greece and Constantinople

Hungerie 101, Hungary

Jerico 242, Jericho
Jerusalem 69, 108, 154, 204, 308
Jhesu 170, 790, **Jhesus** 187, 674, Jesus
Judeus 129, 172 Jew(s)

Karle, 151, 228, 638, **Karles**, 123, 128, 228, 623, **Karleun**, 1, 130, 275, Charlemagne
Karlemaine, 250, 809, 814, 816, 864, **Karlemaines**, 182, 190, 202, Charlemagne

Lalice 103, Lycia or Laodicea (see note to vv. 100-08)
Latanie, la 208, church of St Mary Latin (see note)
Lazare 164, St Lazarus
Loheregne 101, Lorraine

Marie 187, 207, the Virgin Mary
Maseuz 430, the name of a fairy

Naimes 531, **Naimon** 62, one of the twelve peers

Oger de Denemarche 63, **Ogers** 518, one of the twelve peers
Oliver 61, 404, 484, 693, 712, 714, 722, 824, 853, 856, Oliver, Roland's companion and one of the twelve peers
Orenge, see **Willeme (de Orenge)**

Paris 36, 654, 862, **Parys** 60,